Penguin Education

Penguin Science of Behaviour
General Editor: B. M. Foss

Social Psychology
Editor: Michael Argyle

Socialization
Kurt Danziger

Penguin Science of Behaviour

This book is one of an ambitious project, the Penguin Science of Behaviour, which covers a very wide range of psychological inquiry. Many of the short 'unit' texts are on central teaching topics, while others deal with present theoretical and empirical work which the Editors consider to be important new contributions to psychology. We have kept in mind both the teaching divisions of psychology and also the needs of psychologists at work. For readers working with children, for example, some of the units in the field of Developmental Psychology will deal with psychological techniques in testing children, other units will deal with work on cognitive growth. For academic psychologists, there will be units in well-established areas such as Cognitive Psychology, but also units which do not fall neatly under any one heading, or which are thought of as 'applied', but which nevertheless are highly relevant to psychology as a whole.

The project is published in short units for two main reasons. Firstly, a large range of short texts at inexpensive prices gives the teacher a flexibility in planning his course and recommending texts for it. Secondly, the pace at which important new work is published requires the project to be adaptable. Our plan allows a unit to be revised or a fresh unit to be added with maximum speed and minimal cost to the reader.

Above all, for students, the different viewpoints of many authors, sometimes overlapping, sometimes in contradiction, and the range of topics Editors have selected will reveal the complexity and diversity which exist beyond the necessarily conventional headings of an introductory course.

B.M.F.

Contents

Editorial Foreword

This volume is in the Social Psychology section of the Science of Behaviour series. In this part of the series a number of volumes are planned which will give a comprehensive coverage of social psychology, each written by active research workers, and providing an up-to-date and rigorous account of different parts of the subject. There has been an explosive growth of research in social psychology in recent years and the subject has broken out of its early preoccupation with the laboratory to study social behaviour in a variety of social settings. These volumes will differ somewhat from most existing textbooks: in addition to citing laboratory experiments they will cite field studies, and deal with the details and complexities of the phenomena as they occur in the outside world. Links will be established with other disciplines such as sociology, anthropology, animal behaviour, linguistics and other branches of psychology, where relevant. As well as being useful to students, these monographs should therefore be of interest to a wide public – those concerned with the various fields dealt with.

Kurt Danziger has produced a very thoughtful and interesting account of the present state of theory and research concerning socialization. There is a large 'classical' literature, but Danziger is rightly very critical of much of this work. Often it has failed to be replicated: it is now known, for example, that 'dependence', 'aggressiveness', etc. are not unitary traits; mothers are found to be very unreliable reporters of what happens in families; while parents influence children, children also influence parents. The emphasis of more recent research has shifted away from correlational studies to the study of socialization processes and to longitudinal studies. Some continuity is found in *phenotypes*, i.e. the underlying structures which have a common meaning for the agent.

Emphasis is placed in this book on socialization processes such as reinforcement, imitation, early attachment and the effects of two-way relationships in the family. A number of special aspects of socialization are dealt with – the development of sex roles, morals and of cognitive styles and related aspects of personality. The book ends with chapters which place socialization in a wider setting by considering the effect of factors outside the family such as peer groups, differences between social classes, and variations between different cultures and historical periods.

M. A.

Acknowledgement

My wife, Flora, was an active collaborator in the preparation of this volume. While her direct contribution covers chapter 8 and part of chapter 6, the most important part of her influence was too pervasive to be identified by chapter.

1 Recent Origins of the Term 'Socialization'

Although Durkheim and Freud had been deeply concerned with problems of socialization, the use of the term in its modern sense originated in the late 1930s and early 1940s (Clausen, 1968, part 2). In 1939, two prominent scholars, Park and Dollard, independently used the term in the titles of papers published by the *American Journal of Sociology* and in 1940 the influential sociology textbook by Ogburn and Nimkoff devoted several chapters to 'the process whereby the individual is converted into the person', namely, 'socialization'. What is striking is the precise historical synchrony which marks the simultaneous emergence of socialization as a field of study in three disciplines – sociology, anthropology and psychology. In the year in which the articles by Park and Dollard appeared, Kardiner's *The Individual and His Society* was published and two years previously the second edition of Murphy's reference work on *Experimental Social Psychology* was provided with the subtitle: *An Interpretation of Research on the Socialization of the Individual*. The year 1939 also saw the publication of a seminal work on *Frustration and Aggression* by the Yale group of neo-behaviourists and here the term 'socialization' is used in its modern sense in a chapter heading. In view of the rare occurrence of the term in earlier writings in the three disciplines, its sudden emergence to prominence suggests the operation of a powerful undercurrent of ideas.

Let us ask why the old term 'education' would not be adequate to cover the new areas of concern, for it is clear that to some extent its reference is similar to that of the new term. Both terms refer to an active intervention in the life of the individual by social agents who seek to mould him. But the shift from 'education' to 'socialization' expresses a fundamental shift of perspective. It is firstly a shift from an essentially normative perspective to the perspective of a detached observer, a shift from moral philosopher to social scientist. In fact, if 'education' is essentially concerned with the value of goals and techniques, 'socialization' is concerned with their 'how', their effectiveness. It is no longer a question of debating the propriety of educational aims and methods but of describing their diversity and of analysing the processes by which educational influences exert their effect. The implication is clear: the study of 'socialization' excludes the question of the individual's relation to any moral order beyond an actually existing set of social norms and cultural values, and their human agents. In this respect the shift from 'education' to 'socialization' simply recapitulates the general change from social philosophy to positivistic social science.

In practice, the reformulation of educational problems in terms of processes of socialization has also meant a very definite tilting of the balance in favour of society rather than the individual; so much so, in fact, that some contemporary sociologists have felt it necessary to complain of the 'oversocialized conception of man' which prevails in their discipline (Wrong, 1961). The very term 'socialization' seems to posit society as the goal-setter and active principle, leaving the individual as something that is worked upon, more or less successfully. Socialization is usually thought of as something that happens to or is done to the individual – the focus is not on the active shaping of his life by the individual, but on the plasticity and passivity of the individual in the face of social influences. It is this somewhat distorted perspective which is the source of much that is questionable and problematical in current research on socialization – a point to which we shall have occasion to return in later chapters.

Perhaps there is a sense in which the political and the

psychological meaning of the term 'socialization' converge. If the socialization of the means of production arises out of an interest in changing obsolescent social relations, psychological socialization becomes interesting when it is a matter of changing obsolescent individual attitudes. Socialization of the means of production is regarded as a necessity if the essential fetter on economic development is seen to lie in inappropriate social relations, but if the essential obstacle to material progress is located rather in the irrational attitudes of individuals, then it is psychological socialization which counts. Both forms of usage arise out of a concern about the problematic nature of social progress, but the source of inertia is located in the social system, in once case, and in the individual, in the other.

Apparently, the psychological meaning of the term lacks the programmatic overtones of the political meaning. But this is only superficially true. In fact, the earlier forms of socialization theory, which flourished in American anthropology in particular, are structurally very similar to Marxism. Kardiner (1945), the most systematic representative of this trend, sharply distinguishes between the primary and the secondary institutions of society like any good Marxist. But whereas both theories agree in identifying the secondary institutions as cultural and political, Kardiner's primary institutions are the institutions of child training, not the relations of production. For Kardiner, even more than for Marx, the secondary institutions of society have a 'superstructural' character, which means that they are ultimately the product of the primary institutions and cannot be essentially changed without a change in the latter. For Kardiner, most of the institutions of society are a reflection of social or national character which is itself the product of characteristic patterns of child training. It is true that no programme of social action is spelled out, but the implication could hardly be clearer: if you wish to make any real changes in the institutions of society, change your methods of child training.

Such a message was both a response to the peculiar social problems of a society of immigrants and a reflection of the characteristic reception given to the theories of Freud in that society. The migration of families to a different social climate always calls into question the established relationships between parents and children. Rapid social change will usually create tensions between older children and their parents, but the treatment of young children is generally left to undergo slow and silent transformation. It is the actual transplantation of the family to a society with different patterns of child care that leads to an appreciation of the arbitrariness of these patterns. Where this occurs on a mass scale, the shaping of child-care patterns readily becomes a the United States the improvement of parental treatment matter for public discussion and public policy. Indeed, in of infants and young children (as distinct from questions of criminal abuse of parental power) has been accepted as a proper subject for government intervention for over half a century. The Children's Bureau of the Federal Government was organized in 1912 and it has issued its influential publication, *Infant Care*, regularly since 1914. This bulletin, widely circulated among medical and social agencies, contains authoritative statements on the nature of the child and the likely effect of various forms of parental treatment. The moralizing intent of the medium is only thinly covered by a veneer of assumed expertise.

In the context of social problems created by the uneven absorption of immigrants, the relevance of childhood experience is clear. For the adult immigrant, the sources of difficulties in acculturation often do lie in patterns acquired quite early in life, the most obvious being language, and the great plasticity of the young organism is a very striking experience for immigrant parents. From the point of view of social policy, therefore, the period of childhood becomes the primary focus for programmes designed to accelerate the process of acculturation. On the one hand, such policies have made the American school into an agent of the 'melting pot' (Henry, 1963) and, on the other hand, they have produced the swings of fads and fashions characteristic of American parenthood (Bronfenbrenner, 1961a). In such an atmosphere, Freud's emphasis on the fantasies of childhood could easily be interpreted as an emphasis on the treatment received in childhood and so the themes of Freud's account of childhood phantasy have provided the source of many of the earlier theories in this area.

Since the early days of the culture–personality school, represented by Kardiner, Mead and Gorer, the study of socialization has become increasingly separated from matters of public concern. It is now an autonomous field of investigation with its own body of theory and a certain fund of research experience. The process whereby the individual becomes a participating member of a society of human adults is certainly a legitimate subject for objective study and a valuable source of theoretical problems in psychology and sociology.

Nevertheless, it must be said that this field of study bears the marks of its historical origins. On one level this can be seen in a persistent tendency to emphasize the permanent plasticity of human response and to deny the existence of irreversible structural changes in human development. But at a more fundamental level research on socialization has continued to show the influence of what might be called an ideology of social engineering. In reviewing this research it is difficult to escape the impression that much of it has been motivated less by a desire for understanding than by a desire for quick recipes. Again and again the questions to be investigated have been formulated in a manner which suggests that specific manipulations performed on the child were expected to have specific and reliable consequences for his social development. At one stage these critical manipulations were looked for in the context of processes like weaning and toilet training; later they were believed to lie in a few dimensions of parental attitude, like permissiveness or warmth. More recently, the language of social engineering has availed itself of the vocabulary of operant conditioning (Gewirtz, 1969), starting from the correct supposition that it is not always necessary to understand a process in order to develop effective techniques for its social control.

Contrary to this orientation, the present volume will not be concerned with socialization in the sense of techniques for the social control of the individual. It will rather examine a body of theory and of evidence, now growing rather rapidly, which promises to shed new light on some old questions in psychology and the social sciences. In particular, it will explore the different meanings of social participation for child and adult and ask how one form of participation comes to be replaced by another.

special aspects that might be crucial for later life. How can such a selection be made with some reasonable expectation of 'returns' from the time-consuming and often expensive research process?

The selection of categories of adult behaviour felt to be worthy of study has seldom been experienced as a problem. The practical problems of life have always suggested such categories with great insistence. The study of the authoritarian character, at first among the Germans and later also among others, was not the result of any purely scholarly pursuit, it was the result of an essentially political interest. Similarly, the situation where studies on the need for achievement outnumber studies on all other conceivable human needs put together is surely not unrelated to the ideology of entrepreneurship and concern about economic underdevelopment. Again, the social worker, psychiatrist or clinical psychologist, acting as the agent of society, is understandably worried about individual aggressiveness or pathological forms of dependency.

Almost without exception, the categories of human behaviour for which antecedents have been sought in childhood are categories that define current social problems. It is only when we define the problem of Nazism or racialism in terms of its appeal to the authoritarian character that authoritarianism becomes an important research category. Similarly, it is the definition of economic backwardness in terms of deficiencies in entrepreneurship that makes the need for achievement an important problem for psychological investigation. And again, it is our definition of social problems like delinquency and helplessness in psychological terms like aggressiveness and dependency that makes such categories interesting for the potential research worker.

In other words, the categories of adult human behaviour that provided the starting point for many of the earlier studies of socialization were essentially definitions of current social problems. Research in the area of socialization, therefore, frequently became a search for the cause of present problem situations in the childhood antecedents of some of the participants in these situations. Such research is essentially 'applied' research, not motivated by any very profound theoretical questions or elaborate systems of thought.

The major example of this approach is to be found in the voluminous literature on the antecedents of 'dependency' and 'aggressiveness'. These labels have generally been used to identify personality traits whose consistency was far too readily taken for granted. Our interaction with other people is governed by conventions about the limits of acceptable behaviour. When the other individual steps outside those limits we spontaneously blame this on some inherent personal quality of the other or, much more rarely, ourselves. The individual who is seen as being rather more assertive than the situation warrants is labelled 'aggressive', as though the aggressiveness resided in him and not in our relationship. We are apt to forget that in another relationship, perhaps with his wife or mother, this same individual may act in ways we would be more inclined to label 'meek' or 'timid'. Similarly, the child who makes a nuisance of himself by clinging to his teacher and constantly demanding her approval, is likely to be labelled 'dependent', although he may be anything but dependent in other relationships, for instance, with his father or his brother.

The naïve and unreflecting tendency of human beings is to see their interaction in terms of agents endowed with permanent and constant properties (Heider, 1958). As long as we are personally engaged in a relationship, this is a useful way of introducing some order into our experience of other people; it is also a useful way of identifying some of the problems we meet in our daily interaction with others. But if we want to play the role of scientist or psychologist and to gain some knowledge of the other as he really is, we need to step outside the confines of a particular relationship and look at the person in *all* his important social relationships. When we do this, we generally find that what we had taken to be a reliable, general personal quality is no such thing, but only appears in certain types of relationship. We may find that this particular individual earns the label 'aggressive' only from male authority figures and that a particular child is called 'overdependent' only by female teachers. In other words, we have no right to expect that the labels attached to individuals by particular classes of others correspond to any truly general personality characteristics that will reliably manifest themselves no matter what the circumstances.

Occasionally, we do come across such general characteristics, but this is the extreme, and often pathological, case. Because uncontrollably destructive children are known to exist, we cannot conclude that 'aggressiveness' constitutes a general personality trait on which all children can be meaningfully measured. There is no more logic in this procedure than if we wanted to take the existence of albinos as evidence for the existence of a continuous trait of 'albinism', applicable to all individuals. The existence of extreme variants is no indication that the trait in question varies continuously in the population at large – it is at least as likely that the 'extreme case' is qualitatively rather than quantitatively different from individuals classified as normal.

There are good reasons why the characteristics of 'dependency' and 'aggression' have come in for such a large share of attention in the socialization literature. The goal of socialization, as conventionally conceived, is to bring the individual to a proper regard for the limits of desirable and acceptable behaviour in various situations and relationships. The 'oversocialized' individual is commonly regarded as one who treats these limits with an anxious regard that stifles his individuality and creativity. The 'undersocialized' individual is one who frequently oversteps the conventional boundaries by making unreasonable demands on others or by showing a lack of consideration for the rights and feelings of others. In the former case he is likely to be labelled 'overdependent', in the latter case he will be called rude, impolite or, more generally, 'aggressive'. The terms 'dependency' and 'aggression' are used to refer to the commonest problem areas for the agents of society who have to cope with a child that will not accept their definition of the limits of appropriate behaviour. The naïve reaction, as always, is to see this problem as the expression of a personality trait in the child. In other words, dependency and aggression are taken as personality traits; they play rather the same role as 'faults' or 'weakness' of character did for an older moralistic pedagogy. The substitution of terms has had the effect of hiding the moralistic and punitive overtones that were blatant in the older terminology. But these overtones are merely hidden and not removed, for dependency and aggression are anything but value-neutral terms.

Nevertheless, the element of progress lies in the demand that the generality of personality traits must be empirically demonstrable. We are no longer content to accept the naïve assumptions of characterology without test. It makes no sense to look for general antecedents of personality traits in the social background of the child, unless we have first reassured ourselves that we are indeed dealing with general traits. For if traits like dependency and aggression are merely labels applied in particular settings, we would do better to examine these settings than to look for general causal factors in the individual's past.

From this point of view it comes as no surprise to find that attempts to discover the familial antecedents of dependency and aggression in children have generally failed. Even where a single study has reported significant relationships, attempts at replicating such findings have only served to document the mercurial character of the crucial variables. For about a decade, the monograph entitled *Patterns of Child Rearing* by Sears, Maccoby and Levin (1957) served as the major source of data in the field, at least in the American context. But a more recent, equally ambitious attempt to replicate the findings of the earlier study proved to be quite disappointing (Yarrow, Campbell and Burton, 1968). Dependency and aggression were assessed both by interviewing mothers and by teachers' ratings of the same nursery-school children. The overall measures of the child's dependency derived from these two informants correlated only to the extent of 0·29. In other words, if there is a general personality factor involved, it accounts, at best, for less than 10 per cent of the variance in the children studied. For aggression, the corresponding correlation reaches a very similar level, namely, 0·33. On the other hand, the independent ratings of two teachers correlate rather better with each other than either does with the mother's report – the coefficients being 0·47 for dependency and 0·65 for aggression. This suggests that whatever it is that is being measured under these labels has strong relationship-specific components.

However, even this is overstating the case for the generality of these traits. When we look at the answers of mothers and of teachers to specific questions which are all supposed to refer to the same general quality, we find that correlations are not impressive. More important, the mothers were given a questionnaire several months prior to the interview which covered the same questions as were subsequently asked in the interview. The intercorrelations among questionnaire responses were very much lower (between 0·22 and 0·38) than the intercorrelations among interview responses. The reason for this probably lies in the introduction of an additional link in the chain of 'measurement' for interview responses, namely, the coder. The mother's relatively free report in the interview has to be classified or rated on a number of scales before it can be correlated with other measures. This task is performed by a coder who quickly forms an overall impression of a particular parent–child relationship and whose ratings are, therefore, distorted by the 'halo effect' familiar to all psychologists. The higher internal correlations derived from interview material must probably be regarded as a measurement artefact. It is, therefore, not surprising to find that correlations between mothers' questionnaire and mothers' interview responses are uniformly low (0·39 for dependency and 0·29 for aggression).

Other recent studies present a similar picture. For example, a major study reports an attempt at using trained observers to obtain five different measures of dependency behaviour in nursery-school children. The correlations were between —0·24 and +0·23 for boys and —0·03 and +0.71 for girls (Sears, Rau and Alpert, 1965). The same study also attempted to compare reports and observations of direct and indirect aggression at home and at school. The correlations ranged between —0·20 and +0·36.

With so little evidence for the reality of general traits of dependency and aggression it is hardly to be expected that child-rearing antecedents of these traits can be reliably established. Summarizing the available literature on antecedents of dependency, a research group from the U S National Institute of Mental Health states that 'there is evidence of a lack of consistent and statistically significant research results when one inspects information from several studies' (Yarrow, Campbell and Burton, 1968, p. 45). For aggression, similar conclusions are reached. Earlier studies had reported a low positive correlation (0·23) between the child's aggressiveness and maternal permissiveness towards the expression of aggression; in the N I M H study only one of thirty-six correlations relevant to such an association reached statistical significance, an outcome to be expected by chance. Parental punitiveness is shown to be positively associated with reported aggression on the part of the child only when the mother is the source of information both about her own behaviour and the behaviour of her child. Such correlations are of course spurious. They merely show that the mother sees her relationship with the child in relatively consistent terms of hostility and counter-hostility. They tell us nothing about the child's actual behaviour or about its causes.

A somewhat more promising approach to the practical problem of the antecedents of extreme aggressiveness is to isolate this syndrome as qualitatively distinct and to compare the members of this category with relatively normal individuals. McCord, McCord and Howard (1961) did this on the basis of information from teachers, social agencies, ministers, police, Y M C A directors, employers, etc. They picked twenty-four boys whom society had clearly labelled as 'overtly aggressive' and compared them to normal and to conspicuously non-aggressive boys. It became clear that extreme levels of overt aggression were statistically associated with a home environment characterized by several of the following features: at least one of the parents was punitive towards the child, both parents were dissatisfied with their role in life, the parents disagreed about bringing up children and they were not demonstratively affectionate towards each other. Such findings, while intrinsically interesting, do not necessarily have any bearing on the socialization of normal children, except in so far as they strongly suggest the importance of the relationship between the parents as an antecedent in the socialization process. This is a factor that does not appear to have received the attention it deserves in studies of socialization that lack a clinical perspective.

Longitudinal continuity

The trouble with 'social problem' definitions of psychological categories is that they concentrate on the meaning of human actions for everyone except the agent. What is regarded as aggressive behaviour by others may not be so regarded by the individual and, conversely, an individual may so disguise his aggressiveness that few people would notice it. Similarly, the aggressiveness of two individuals may be equally annoying for others but spring from very different roots in the two cases. Therefore, one would hardly expect to find the same childhood antecedents in both instances. Human behaviour is charactertistically ambiguous. Two people may perform the same action for totally different reasons. It makes a difference whether a boy is aggressive because he wants to demonstrate his masculinity or because he wants to repay someone for wrongs done to him. What appears on the surface is the *phenotype*, what lies beneath is the *genotype* (Lewin, 1935).

We cannot expect to find systematic and reliable relationships between childhood experiences and phenotypical behaviour. Such behaviour is situationally determined and its study is of no value in predicting behaviour under different circumstances. What we would like to be able to do is to trace some relatively stable characteristics of the person to earlier experiences. Such stable characteristics are likely to be genotypical and to express themselves in different ways in different situations.

The first problem for any theory of socialization, then, is to come to a decision about what it is trying to explain. Is it attempting to account for surface patterns of behaviour or for underlying structures? In many cases the existence of the genotype is denied implicitly by an exclusive concern with surface behaviour in specific situations. For other theories, the nature of the psychological structure which is the product of socialization becomes a matter of considerable importance. Broadly speaking, it is the psychoanalytically derived theories and the cognitively oriented theories for which the product of socialization is some kind of genotypical structure, while behaviouristic approaches restrict themselves to relating situation-specific responses to earlier learning.

The way in which one answers the question about the nature of the product of socialization usually determines the selection of those aspects of childhood experience that are felt to be relevant to later behaviour. If it is a matter of predicting situation-specific responses, earlier analogues of the relevant situations will be sought. Thus, the sources of individual differences among adults in regard to such traits as aggressiveness or dependency will be looked for in differences among mothers in handling manifestations of aggression or dependency in the child.

On the other hand, if the process of socialization leaves its precipitate in the form of underlying genotypical structures, then the important childhood experiences are those which create these structures. For example, the antecedents of a structure like that of the 'anal character' may be sought in toilet training. Much of the early work on socialization was, in fact, inspired by psychoanalytic theories of psychic structure and concentrated aspects of childhood experience that were apparently related to Freud's stages of psychosexual development. For example, fixation at the anal level could be seen as the outcome of particularly severe frustration of anal eroticism due to very early and severe toilet training. One would then look for correlations between these aspects of childhood experience and the adult traits that define the 'anal character'.

During the last ten years or so, there has been growing dissatisfaction with the research strategies just described. On the whole, the results of the older studies have been disappointing. In spite of a large research literature, few consistent findings emerge which relate childhood experience to adult behaviour. This is not surprising where purely phenotypical studies are concerned. On the other hand, structural theories are not designed to predict individual differences in biological or psychological function. The most careful macroscopic and microscopic description of the anatomical structures involved in the function of digestion, for example, will not enable us to make any predictions relating *individual differences* in anatomy to individual differences in digestive function. Similarly, Freud's account whch purports to describe certain universal psychological structures involved in the psychological functioning of the personality in general does not logically lead to predictions about individual differences and it does not seem that Freud thought it could ever do so (Freud, 1933).

Many of the more fundamental problems of the older

approach had their source, as we have seen, in the tendency to define socialization essentially in terms of its effects. But the best that can be hoped for in that direction is a little more light on some vexing social problems. No advance in our understanding of the fundamentals of human behaviour is likely to follow, because no fundamental questions are being asked. The old research paradigm is satisfied with the establishment of correlations; it is not adequate as a test of theoretical ideas, because the absence of correlation may mean no more than an invalid procedure and the presence of a correlation yields no information about possible causal relationships. Supposing that severity of toilet training were indeed related to anal character traits in the adult, which it is not, then we are still left with two additional possibilities: the previously existing obstinacy of the child provoked the severe attempts at training by the mother, or the mother's manner of toilet training and the child's character traits are both the result of some third, undetected factor emanating from the child, the mother or their common environment.

The best empirical studies in this area seem to offer some support for one of these interpretations. Thus, while no relationship was found between retrospective reports of severity of toilet training and anal character traits, there was a clear correlation between the self-reported presence of these traits in the mother and her adult offspring (Beloff, 1957). In other words, a trait like 'orderliness' may be the result of direct teaching and/or imitation, and if an association with toilet training were found it would simply show that the mother's orderliness manifests itself in this area as it does in many others.

Faced with such considerations, some investigators have turned to the study of socialization as a process rather than as an effect. Their interest has shifted from the products of socialization to its mechanisms. When posed in this way, the questions loses its link to social problems. Therefore, the aspects of behaviour that come under scrutiny are more likely to be defined in terms of their relevance to individual psychological development rather than in terms of their importance for others. In terms of research design, the cross-sectional investigation of individual or natural group differences is replaced by longitudinal studies. It is the only way in which we are likely to discover individual patterns which are stable enough to permit a meaningful search for antecedents in earlier experience. Even if the kinds of behaviour discussed earlier in this chapter turned out to be consistent across situations, which they are not, they may still lack real stability over any significant period of time. For example, in one study of nursery-school boys observed aggression at three and a half years correlated not at all ($r = 0.08$) with observed aggression at five years. Similarly, passive-dependent behaviour in boys of three has been shown to have little or no relationship to passive-dependent behaviour at age ten (Kagan, 1969). In the absence of longitudinal continuity it would be pointless to continue the search for the antecedents of such ephemeral patterns of behaviour.

But longitudinal studies also provide a basis for modest optimism. While phenotypical traits lack developmental continuity, there is clear evidence for a kind of continuity that is psychologically meaningful. For example, in one study, nursery-school children were observed over four school terms (Emmerich, 1964). It was found that children who were somewhat aggressive and outgoing at the beginning of the period became socially poised and non-aggressive later, while children who started off by being labelled 'cooperative' became socially insecure and awkward. While there is no continuity of phenotypical behaviour, it is possible to interpret these results in terms of an underlying genotypical continuity. It may be that these children differed in a stable and consistent way in regard to their trust of adults or anxiety about adult acceptance. Those who trusted adults may have been regarded as somewhat overassertive at first, but later their basic confidence earned them a more desirable label, whereas the anxious children were regarded as cooperative at first because of their obvious desire to please, but later their basic insecurity became apparent.

Social reinforcement

The persistent failure of attempts to identify consistent personality dispositions like aggressiveness or dependency has led some investigators to approach the problem of socialization by studying highly particular, situation-specific reactions in the laboratory. In this view, socialization is the product of the 'reinforcement history' of the individual in particular situations (Bijou, 1970). A reinforcement is any event whatever that makes more probable a response which it precedes or follows with some regularity. In the former case we have the paradigm of classical (respondent) conditioning and, in the latter case, the paradigm of operant conditioning. Reinforcing events include certain stimulus–response sequences, stimulus deprivations, response sets and a multitude of other conditions. Such events, to be effective, are generally thought to require some regularity in their occurrence; such regularities are termed 'schedules of reinforcement'.

The establishment of a reinforcement history involves an analysis of the individual's situation in the following terms: (a) an identification of those aspects of the situation which have demonstrable effects on the behaviour of the individual (the 'stimulus'); (b) an identification of certain of the individual's movement patterns in terms of their effects or results (the 'response'); (c) an identification of reinforcers as defined above; and (d) an account of the temporal patterning of reinforcers (the 'reinforcement schedule').

Two fundamental characteristics of this approach are its purely descriptive nature (no assumptions are made about what causes an event to become a 'stimulus' or a 'reinforcement') and the highly specific reference of these descriptions. The more global the definition of stimulus, response and reinforcement become in a given case, the more closely these descriptive categories resemble the phenomenal categories of the naïve description of human actions which we all use in everyday life (Heider, 1958). Any advance over this level of description depends on the greater specificity of reference which the social reinforcement paradigm encourages.

The combination of its purely descriptive nature and the highly specific reference of its terms produces a critical problem of generality for this approach. If the account of the reinforcement history is to have any significance beyond the unique combination of circumstances operating for a particular individual in specific situations, some generalizations about the operation of reinforcement contingencies must be established. Typically, laboratory studies have been used to establish such generalizations. Many of these studies have used animal rather than human subjects, on the assumption that ultimately the same principles apply to human socialization and to animal learning under laboratory conditions.

Except that stimuli occurring in natural settings are likely to be more variable than stimuli in contrived laboratory experiments, and that the term social stimuli usually denotes those occurring in natural settings, there is nothing intrinsically special about stimuli provided by people or about social settings as contexts for learning. Thus, the term 'social learning' simply defines a category of learning that involves stimuli provided by people but that follows the same principles as nonsocial learning (Gewirtz, 1969).

The 'principles of non-social learning' which reinforcement theorists have in mind are those which they believe to have been established by the observation of caged animals under highly restricted conditions. In the classical animal learning experiment the experimenter is in complete control of the stimulus conditions, the reinforcement contingencies and the response options available to the experimental subject. In learning experiments with children an attempt has usually been made to replicate these conditions. This has meant that all interpretations of socialization in terms of social reinforcement have shared a common model of the child as an essentially passive organism under the control of a socializing agent who dispenses rewards and punishments (Zigler and Child, 1969). This preconception led to a neglect of those factors contributing to the course of socialization which are not under the control of external agents. Such factors include maturational processes which predetermine the sequence and structure of developmental stages, as well as hereditary and congenital conditions. Among the psychologically relevant functions for which clear individual differences have been demonstrated in early infancy are autonomic response patterns, social responsiveness, sleeping and feeding patterns, sensory thresholds, motility and perceptual responses (Thomas, 1963).

The one truly impressive finding of studies of social reinforcement has its source in the repeated demonstration of the fact that the reinforcing function of a given event depends entirely on the social context in which it occurs. As Solomon (1964) expresses it when speaking of negative reinforcers: 'A punishment is not just a punishment. It is an event in the temporal and spatial flow of stimulation and behaviour, and its effects will be produced by its temporal and spatial point of insertion in that flow.' (Perhaps there is a certain historical irony in the fact that learning theory is by way of becoming the Gestalt psychology of rewards.) The rewarding or inhibiting effects of simple expressions of approval or disapproval ('good', 'no', etc.) have been shown to vary with the sex of the experimenter, the sex, age, social class and race of the child and the preceding experimental procedure (Stevenson, 1965). Similar observations apply to the effects of the experimenter's silence. Moreover, conditions which produce one kind of effect in the laboratory can produce different, and sometimes opposite, effects outside it.

The attempt to explain socialization in terms of social reinforcement, that is to say, patterns of rewards and punishment disbursed by parents or other controlling agents, is based on a model of human learning that has so far provided few, if any, demonstrably valid generalizations about the effects of child rearing. This model proposes that people learn only as a result of specific reinforcements for discrete acts. However, over the past decade a very large number of experimental studies have demonstrated what everyone else always knew, namely, that people learn from each other by observation and that the direct experience of 'reinforcement' is usually unnecessary for the modification of human behaviour. There is overwhelming evidence that children learn complex acts through cognitive processes based on observation rather than through being trained by external reinforcements administered by the parent. This does not mean that the reward and punishment of specific components of behaviour plays *no* role in social learning; it does mean that that role is defined in a context provided by the very special reactions that people have to people. These reactions require more detailed discussion in a separate chapter.

3 Learner and Model

The experimental study of imitative behaviour has produced quite a major shift of emphasis in the psychological literature on socialization. Over the last decade the phenomenon of learning by observation has become the major focus of experimental research in this area.

In an early study of this type (Bandura, 1965a) nursery-school children were exposed to an adult who spent several minutes mistreating a doll by sitting on it, punching it, pummelling it with a mallet and kicking it about the room. After this, they were allowed to become involved in some attractive toys, only to be told that the experimenter had changed her mind and had decided to reserve the use of these toys for some other children. This frustrating experience, obviously designed to instigate aggressive behaviour, was followed by the experimentally presented opportunity in the form of a doll similar to the one whose mistreatment had recently been witnessed by the child, as well as a mallet, dart guns, etc. In order to allow for some choice about the display of aggressive behaviour, ordinary toys like cars, animals, crayons, a ball and a tea-set were also available for the child's use. The aggression displayed by the child over a twenty-minute period was rated by unseen observers who distinguished carefully between imitative aggression that closely followed the behaviour of the adult model and non-imitative aggression that involved actions not previously observed by the child in the experimental situation. When the behaviour of these children was compared with that of others in a control group not previously exposed to the aggressive actions of an adult model, they were found to have taken over many of the actions of the model. They often set about kicking, punching and pummelling the doll, whereas such behaviour was quite rare among the children in the control group.

In order to use the language of operant conditioning to interpret the results obtained in experiments where children observe and imitate adult models, it is necessary to assume the existence of previously learned generalized imitative responses. This definitely excludes the possibility that *novel* responses may have been learned by the child's observation of the model. For instance, in the experiment described previously, no specific reward is administered to the child for taking over the behaviour of the model. But a pure stimulus–response theory can allow for the acquisition of new responses only in cases where external control or 'reinforcement' exists. Hence, the child's imitative aggression must be traced to some hypothetical events in his past which did involve external control of responses by means of differential reinforcement. This means that the language of operant conditioning is not at all helpful when we try to give an account of what might be happening in most instances of social learning that occur either in real life or in an experimental setting. The trouble is that this language contains no terms that refer to processes specific to the situation where one person learns something from another.

The only theories which can properly be called theories of *social* learning are those which contain terms that refer to the mediating function of symbols. In experimental situations, children who have observed a model exhibit novel patterns of aggressive response not only imitate these actions but are also able to describe them verbally with a rather high degree of accuracy. It is assumed that images and symbolic representations of the model's behaviour persist after the responses they represent.

Some evidence for the function of symbolic processes in observational learning is provided by an experiment in which the children were asked to reproduce the actions of a model after they had observed them on a film (Bandura, Ross and Ross, 1963a). The actions were somewhat unusual, in fact slightly bizarre, so that they would be truly novel responses for the children who repeated them. The model would be shown entering the room with one hand cupped over his eyes, he would throw bean bags through his legs with his back to the target, then he would retrieve the bags, pace backwards, squat with his back to the target and throw a bean bag over each shoulder. His other actions were also designed to present the child with response sequences that he was most unlikely to have carried out in the past. One group of children simply watched the filmed actions of the model passively, a second group was asked to verbalize these actions as they saw them on the screen, and a third group was asked to count while they watched the film. As expected, the second group later reproduced the actions of the model most fully and the third group put in the worst performance when asked to match the model's behaviour. In the second group, observational learning was facilitated by the appropriate symbolic representation, while the group that had to count while watching the model was hampered by interfering symbolization. The mediating role of symbolic processes in observational learning has, therefore, been clearly demonstrated.

The limits of nurturance

Children do not imitate everyone indiscriminately. Only certain persons are honoured by being taken as models and even then they are given this status only on certain occasions. A child may readily learn a skill from one person and resist strongly the attempts of others to teach him. What is the magic that makes one adult an admired hero and another a hateful nuisance?

There is a kind of psychological folk-lore which attributes the effectiveness of models to their 'warmth' or nurturance. The person who takes care of the child's needs and offers him plenty of affection is supposed to achieve a special status in the child's regard. That person's approval becomes crucial to the child and his or her actions become worthy of imitation. While it is true that in experimental situations a friendly adult is more likely to be imitated than an unfriendly one (Mischel and Grusec, 1966), the evidence from field studies is contradictory. The major source of evidence here comes from studies of sex-role identification, that is, the tendency of girls to imitate their mothers and boys to imitate their fathers. At least one important study of sex-typed behaviour in nursery-school children finds no indication that either the mothers of feminine girls or the fathers of masculine boys were particularly distinguished by the warmth of their relationship with the child or by their tendency to use a love-oriented approach to discipline (Sears, Rau and Alpert, 1965).

There is certainly no clear and simple relationship between the readiness of the child to adopt a given adult as a model and that adult's degree of warmth or nurturance. It may well be that once a certain minimum level of nurturance has been established, this fact becomes essentially irrelevant to the socialization process. It may also be that the functional relationship between nurturance and readiness to imitate the model has the shape of an inverted U, with both highly nurturant and highly depriving adults being essentially failures as models. In any case, an examination of the research literature in this area suggests that there is no direct proportionality between the 'warmth' of the model and tendency to imitate (Aronfreed, 1969).

Another possibility is that the child reacts to changes in the level of nurturance rather than to the level itself. He may be motivated to accept a given model because of the threat of withdrawal of nurturance or affection. In that case, it would not be love but the fear of its loss which would motivate the child to perform the socially approved action. The parent who employs the actual or threatened withdrawal of love as a device for getting the child to follow him is really using his position as the child's caretaker as a source of power. What the child reacts to in this case is the power which the parent's nurturant role gives him, not the nurturance itself. It is necessary to consider this factor separately, for there is a great deal of research which attests to the importance of power in the modelling process.

Qualities of the model

Some models appear to have an almost irresistible power over children, others are ignored. What is the source of such power?

The literature of psychology contains a number of suggestions for answering this question. While modelling undoubtedly occurs under a wide variety of conditions, the most important task for research is to discover the necessary and sufficient conditions for its occurrence. For example, being the recipient of valued resources does not in itself make a model compelling. It had seemed plausible to some (Whiting, 1960) that the child might model himself on those whose status allows them to consume those desired rewards of which the child feels himself to be deprived. The boy, therefore, imitates his father because the latter is the privileged recipient of the mother's love. However, it has been shown that at least in the psychological laboratory children tend to imitate the person who is the source of desirable objects, like attractive toys and foods, rather than the person who competes with them for these rewards (Bandura, Ross and Ross, 1963b). While this observation by no means excludes the applicability of the 'status envy' theory to real life family settings, it does at least indicate that envy is neither a necessary nor a sufficient condition for the occurrence of modelling.

Whiting's 'status envy' theory is, of course, a reinterpretation of Freud's oedipal theory. The original theory had stressed the threatening qualities of the model rather than its position as a rival or competitor. Anna Freud's term, 'identification with the aggressor', expresses the suggestion that imitation may function as a defence against anxiety generated by a threatening power figure. While this may be true on occasion, it describes neither the necessary nor the sufficient conditions for the occurrence of the process, because in the laboratory both adults and children readily imitate aggressive models who present no threat to them whatever (Walters and Thomas, 1963).

As usual, experimenters and clinicians are at cross purposes. What clinically inspired theories generally try to do is to make sense out of certain instances of odd behaviour known to occur in real life. They do not generally make explicit claims about the supposed universality of their generalizations, but neither do they specify the special conditions under which these generalizations apply. It is, then, a simple matter for the experimentalist to construct an artificial situation in which the theories of the clinician clearly do not apply. This merely shows the original generalizations to lack the universality which had never been claimed for them. A more productive use of the experimental method would be involved in the search for the specific conditions under which the clinical generalizations might apply. In practice, this type of research is seldom regarded as worthwhile; instead, we get a search for the necessary and the sufficient conditions for the occurrence of the phenomenon under study.

Sometimes, the evidence from everyday experience is so clear that further experimental illustrations would be trivial. For instance, one hardly needs elaborate documentation to know that children and adolescents will readily take as models figures with whom they have not interacted at all. Pop singers and the heroes of organized sport will be imitated, even though they do not interact with their admirers in any direct way. Therefore, it is not only unnecessary for the model to be a threat to his follower, it is not even necessary for him to have any kind of control over the follower. It is *observation* of the model and not interaction with the model that is necessary for social learning to occur.

But if observation of the model is necessary, it is certainly not a sufficient condition for imitation. Many persons' acts are observed but not copied. One possibility is that it is only the acts of *successful* models that are imitated. Indeed, there are a number of experiments which show that the aggressive actions of a model are more likely to be copied when they are rewarded and less likely to be copied when they are punished (Bandura, 1969). But the interpretation of these experiments is difficult. When a child copies the behaviour of an adult, we can only infer the occurrence of social *learning* if we are certain that this behaviour was not already in the child's repertoire before the experimental adult model appeared on the scene. Let us take the case where the copied action consists of punching a doll. If the child has punched a doll before, he has not really learned anything – all that the adult did was to indicate to the child that it was permissible to punch dolls in this setting. In other words, the effect was on the *performance* of previously learned acts rather than on the *learning* of new acts. In that case, it would be more correct to regard the adult as the releaser of the child's behaviour rather than as its model. There is no doubt that successful example can release similar previously learned behaviour, but it is an open question whether it is in itself enough to induce the learning of new responses. Because it is obviously impossible to prove that a particular child has no previous familiarity with a particular class of actions, one has to rely on plausibility. This means that alternative interpretations of experiments on observational learning are always possible, though in any given instance they may appear to be rather far-fetched.

In some cases it is unnecessary to assume that it was the social *power* of the model that induced imitation. The perception of power is only possible on the basis of a fairly advanced level of cognitive development. But Piaget (1951) and others have shown that infants less than one year old regularly imitate interesting activities of other people. This is itself an outgrowth of the infant's tendency to repeat his own activities in the form of what Piaget calls 'circular reactions'. In due course, the perceived activities of others are substituted for the infant's own activities. This is a fairly primitive tendency and does not depend on the child's special relationship to the model or on the perception of the latter's social power. A good deal of observational learning produced in experimental situations may involve no more than this primitive mechanism and explanations in terms of the special qualities of the model may in fact be redundant.

Personal and positional modelling

The source of the power of models which are considered worth imitating is elusive. It is not, as we have seen, necessarily a matter of direct power over the follower himself, nor can we be sure that it is simply a matter of demonstrated success. At this stage it may help to make a distinction between two kinds of models, personal models and positional models. A personal model is followed for the sake of his personal attributes, a positional model for the sake of the attributes that pertain to his social position as defined by sex, age, occupation, etc. (Winch, 1962). What the child enacts when imitating a positional model is a social role, not a personal style. In the psychological laboratory a male experimenter serving as model represents not only himself, but also men in general, and his behaviour may say to the child, 'Act like a man', rather than, 'Act like me.' So it is not surprising to find that the aggressive behaviour of male models is more readily copied than the aggressive behaviour of female models. Aggressiveness is more acceptable as part of the male role. In imitating male aggressiveness the child remains within the limits of a role pattern that is well known to him, but taking over aggressiveness from a female would involve a more personal imitation that is much less likely to occur under laboratory conditions which exclude close personal familiarity with the model.

The conditions governing these two kinds of modelling may well be different. For example, familiarity, based on previous interaction with the model, may well be crucial for personal models but it is clearly not important for positional models, where it is only a question of the child being familiar with the social role in general. Again, it seems likely that an individual's capacity for threatening the child, either by the withdrawal of nurturance or by some active form of punishment, may help to instate him as a personal rather than as a positional model. This may explain the common clinical pattern where imitation of an aggressive and punitive father is associated with an extremely weak internalization of the male role in general. Clinical theories and experimental tests have been at cross purposes, because while the former have been mainly concerned with personal modelling, the latter have involved conditions that are much more likely to evoke positional modelling. Hence it is extremely difficult to produce experimental evidence for the occurrence of imitation as a defensive reaction. The necessary conditions for such 'defensive identification', as described by clinicians, involve the combination of great familiarity and threat, a combination that has yet to be reproduced in the laboratory. The claim of the clinician that modelling may fulfil defensive functions therefore retains a strong basis of plausibility, but the conditions under which this happens need to be more precisely described.

What is involved in positional modelling is not the model's direct power over the child, as in the case of personal modelling, but the model's perceived status in the social system of which both he and the child are parts. The child may be merely a spectator, but he is impressed by a model that demonstrates his control over valued resources, even though the child may not benefit directly from this control. The kind of power that inheres in a social position is different from the personal aggressiveness or punitiveness of an individual. The former is *legitimized* power that implies the existence of a normative framework which the child accepts.

We must, therefore, stress the need for drawing a clear

distinction between two kinds of power and the two kinds of modelling related to them. The power of a personal threat to the child is not the same as the power that comes from the control of resources in some social system. Clinical evidence seems to suggest that the first kind of power may lead to imitation as a form of psychological defence, and the experimental evidence clearly illustrates the effectiveness of positional power in inducing modelling effects. But the modelling or imitation that takes place is not the same in these two situations. If the source of a model's power is perceived to lie in his personal attributes, then he will be imitated as an individual, but if the source of power inheres in the position the model occupied in a social system, then he will be imitated as a representative of that position. While familiarity is an important condition of the first type of modelling, similarity between the present or expected role of follower and model is more important for the second type of modelling. It is also clear that the differentiation between an individual and the social position he represents will appear only at a certain level of cognitive development, that is, when the child is able to distinguish clearly between a category and one of its individual members. When that stage is reached the child commonly adopts new models that represent social rather than individual power. The shift from mother to father and to teacher may well be the outcome of such a development.

A crucial factor for positional modelling is the relevance of the role of the model for that of the child. Boys are more likely to imitate the aggressiveness of male models than are girls. The child needs to see some similarity betweeen himself and the model in order to take over some of the behaviour of the model.

The selective imitation of models of the same sex, for example, is based on a categorization of oneself as belonging to a fixed-gender class. The behaviour of other members of this class then appears as more appropriate to oneself than the behaviour of members of the opposite-gender class.

Until the child's cognitive development has reached a level where such categorization is possible, no preferential imitation of models of the same sex takes place. The criteria for establishing similarity became more specific with age – a very young child may imitate a dog or a cat – so that the developmental changes in positional modelling are parallel to the changes in self-definition. As the child's cognitive capacity becomes greater, so he comes to use more abstract status dimensions for defining social positions. At an early stage the dimensions to which he responds are physicalistic, they involve strength and movement, but later they become more subjective, involving intellectual and moral differences. At age four to five, fathers are perceived as bigger and stronger than mothers, but social power and prestige are not clearly typed in favour of the father until a year or two later (Kohlberg and Zigler, 1967).

A special feature of positional modelling derives from the fact that social roles do not exist separately from each other but are defined by their mutual relationship. Thus, the conventional definition of masculine and feminine roles is not arbitrary but depends on a conception of their complementarity; similarly for roles like buyer and seller, teacher and student, etc. This means that the expectations of those in complementary roles become powerful factors in the adoption of appropriate role patterns. Role-appropriate behaviour is, therefore, not necessarily due to the imitation of appropriate role models; it may be the result of an adaptation to the expectations of people in the complementary role position. This is nicely illustrated by some curious facts about the development of sex-role behaviour. The only clearly demonstrated relationship between the sex-role attitudes of parents and their daughters is that the father's masculinity and his expectations for femininity are correlated with the girl's femininity. Similarly, the rather slight effects of father absence on the masculinity of boys seem to point, among other things, to the importance of the complementary role expectations of the mother.

In the development of the individual, is personal modelling a prerequisite for positional modelling? Is it necessary to identify with a particular example of masculinity or femininity before one can adopt a masculine or feminine role? The problem is important, for it forces us to question the significance of the individual parent in the development of the child. The common-sense view, shared by almost all clinicians and social learning theorists, is that the child's experience with a particular mother or father critically determines the nature of his subsequent learning of social roles. While this may be true if the behaviour of the parents falls outside certain fairly wide limits, it is not necessarily true for the average child of normal parents. In fact, almost all the evidence based on group data rather than individual case histories seems to point to the fact that modelling or adoption of a general social role is largely independent of the effects produced by individual parents.

The major body of evidence in this field comes from studies of the development of masculinity in boys (Kohlberg, 1966). There appears to be only a slight correlation between measures of masculinity and measures of father identification, and no correlation at all between the boy's sex-typing and that of his father. More convincing, in view of the questionable nature of these measures, is the fact that in developmental studies the preferential imitation of strange males occurs no later than the imitation of the father in a projective test. Moreover, a clear preference for sex-typed activities and peers definitely precedes imitation of the father doll in a doll play test. Most important of all, the existing studies of the effect of father absence on the masculinity of boys allow of no definite conclusion. While there is a curious tendency for many authors to quote only those studies which show lowered masculinity in boys without present fathers there are other, equally valid, studies which failed to find this effect. Moreover, the reported effects are typically quite limited and in many instances can be traced to other, uncontrolled variables characterizing father-absent homes. It is, therefore, by no means certain that the adoption of an appropriate sex role depends on a special relationship with a particular parent figure. Such a relationship may facilitate positional identification but it is neither a necessary nor a sufficient condition for its occurrence.

4 The Significance of Sex-Typing

The sex-linked character of behavioural continuity emerges as the most striking finding in a major longitudinal study of personality development (Kagan and Moss, 1962). A group of men and women who had been intensively observed as children were interviewed in their early twenties while records of their behaviour from birth to fourteen were independently assessed. Aggressive behaviour in the early school years predicted similar behaviour for young adult males but not for females. Conversely, passive-dependent behaviour showed some continuity for females but none for males. What does this mean?

A clue to the answer is provided by the relevance of sex-role standards to aggressive and dependent behaviour. Men are expected to show more of the former and women more of the latter. Therefore, it appears that longitudinal continuity is obtained for overt behaviour patterns that correspond to sex-role standards. In fact, the tendency to adopt behaviour patterns congruent with sex-role standards was stable from the early school years to adulthood ($r = 0.63$ for men and 0.44 for women). That we are getting close to some form of genotypic continuity in this area is shown by two curious observations: those males who had reacted passively to stress as boys did not show any tendency to do so as adults, but they did avoid competitive activities and vocations, and adopted interests that were not in line with conventional standards of masculinity. Conversely, those females who were aggressive in the early school years did not remain so, but as adults they were more likely to be 'masculine' in their interests and highly motivated in the direction of intellectual achievement. These observations suggest that when action tendencies conflict with sex-role standards they are likely to find expression in alternative actions which are socially more acceptable. The genotypic continuity is provided by the degree to which the individual is committed to the sex-role standards prescribed by his community.

It should be noted that the contrast between phenotypic and genotypic continuity applies not only to the child but also to the parents. In the past, it has too readily been assumed that parental behaviour was simply a product of parental attitudes and motives. In fact, the child imposes constraints on parental behaviour in much the same way that the parent constrains the overt behaviour of the child. Additional constraints are imposed by culturally imposed standards for the mother and father role. While there have been very few attempts to study the longitudinal continuity of maternal behaviour, such evidence as we do have suggests the importance of social norms. Because warmth and affection towards the offspring are central to the maternal role, it is not surprising to find just these maternal characteristics to be stable from infancy through the pre-adolescence of the child (Schaefer and Bayley, 1963). As no other aspect of maternal behaviour showed any such continuity we might well suspect that the underlying personality variable is once again one of role acceptance, this time of the feminine, maternal role.

In view of the very small number of longitudinal studies for which this kind of information is available, it is of great interest to note that there is another study in which sex-role acceptance emerges as the easiest personality variable to predict (Escalona and Heider, 1959). This time, observations made during the first eight months of life were compared with behaviour in the pre-school period. The authors of the study observe that all the variables for which predictions from infancy to childhood were good were strongly under environmental control. As the research worker was well acquainted with the norms and expectations operating in the milieu, she was probably predicting the conformity of overt behaviour to social norms. It is quite possible that sex-role acceptance is merely one expression of an even more basic genotypical pattern, namely, the tendency to accept or to resist socially imposed rules and pressures. Our conventional definitions of 'masculinity' and 'femininity' involve clear stereotypes of this kind. The male is expected to be independent and aggressive, the female, dependent and accommodating. If we bear in mind these stereotypes it becomes possible to make sense of a number of relevant research findings in this area. One major socialization study (Sears, Rau and Alpert, 1965) finds that a generally non-permissive and punitive attitude on the part of mothers inhibits certain aspects of 'masculinity' in boys but promotes 'femininity' in girls. What seems to happen is that severe socialization pressures produce an 'oversocialized', compliant individual. By certain culturally toned definitions, the behaviour of such an individual is likely to be judged more appropriate to the female than to the male role.

One interesting aspect of these sex-role stereotypes is that the 'feminine' pattern requires continued feedback from the social environment to a greater extent than does the 'male' pattern. It is difficult to assess one's success at being accommodating and pleasing without the appropriate recognition from others. However, in so far as the 'masculine' sex-role stereotype is defined in terms of the independent mastery of cognitive and motor skills, it is more appropriate to judge performance against objective standards rather than direct social feedback. Perhaps this has something to do with the fact that the father's expectations appear to play a particularly important role in the development of the girl's femininity (Mussen and Rutherford, 1963). He provides an important and early source of the kind of feedback needed for effective feminine role identification.

The ubiquity and effectiveness of sex-role stereotypes is impressive. As early as the age of two, there are quite clear sex differences in 'aggressiveness' and 'fearfulness' as well as differences in the interest value of toys. These differences are the product of a complex interaction between innate predispositions and the differential treatment which mothers typically give to male and female infants. However, it is still a big step from these early differences to the deliberate adoption of sex-role stereotypes in later life. Typically, sex-role appropriate behaviour and interests become more and more preponderant and consistent as the individual develops, and in girls, in particular, the final adoption of the appropriate role may be considerably delayed. Early sex differences involve specific activities and interests, whereas at a later stage a general sex-role norm or standard modifies almost everything the individual does.

It is difficult to accept the suggestion that this development is simply the result of preferential reinforcement of sex-appropriate behaviour by parents and others. For one thing, the permanent effectiveness of social reinforcement in older children depends on what the child considers appropriate for himself; it presupposes a previous definition of oneself as a person who engages in such and such behaviour. Normal boys do not need much social reinforcement to adopt new forms of acceptably 'masculine' activity, but it is well nigh impossible to devise an effective reinforcement for actions that would be considered 'effeminate'. Sex-role adoption is as much the 'cause' of social reinforcement as the other way around. Explanations of sex-typing solely in terms of social reinforcement therefore appear to beg the question (Mischel, 1970).

In addition, the research evidence provides considerable difficulties for a simple explanation of sex-typing in terms of differential reinforcement of sex-appropriate behaviour. On the whole, the evidence that dependent behaviour is more frequently rewarded for girls and assertive behaviour more frequently rewarded for boys is equivocal and somewhat inconsistent. Moreover, longitudinal studies using different measures of masculinity and femininity show an irregular and generally low pattern of intercorrelations among these measures. The tests used involve sex-typed attitudes and interests, including toys, as well as projective measures of preferential identification with male or female figures represented by dolls or pictures. If sex-role learning proceeds by a process of continuous differential reinforcement, one might expect a steady and converging development of sex-appropriate behaviour on these tests. In fact, intercorrelations among different measures are somewhat higher among children than among adolescents and adults. In addition, the age trends are highly irregular: at some ages sex-appropriate responses increase, at others they decrease; at some ages there are sudden shifts. Finally, there is little correlation between the masculinity–femininity scores of the same individual at different ages. While the validity of these measures may be questioned (Reed and Asbjornsen, 1968), the total picture is difficult to reconcile with a view of sex-role learning as based solely on a process of continuous social reinforcement of sex-appropriate behaviour.

This somewhat confusing picture can be explained only if we assume that there are several processes at work. Firstly, there is undoubtedly *some* reinforcement of specific sex-typed interests and activities; the vast difference in the toys offered to little boys and the toys offered to little girls hardly allows one to doubt this. But this is a different matter from a *conception* of sex-role stereotypes which function as standards of evaluation or comparison for the individual. It is significant that there is little or no correlation in adults between the actual sex-typing of their interests and their judgement of their own degree of masculinity and feminity. It is possible for a man with typically masculine interests to doubt his own masculinity. The formation of sex-role stereotypes begins rather later and continues rather longer than the specific reinforcement of certain activities and interests. The adoption of an appropriate sex-role *identity* sometimes lags many years behind the development of specific sex-typed behaviours. A girl may happily play with dolls, while still expressing a preference for being a boy.

Gender identity

Both sex-typed interests and sex-role identities appear to depend quite heavily on a third factor which has been called 'gender identity'. In order for the girl to adopt a feminine sex-role identity she must first of all classify herself as a girl, and in order for social reinforcement of sex-typed behaviour to be effective in the long run the behaviour in question must be seen as being appropriate for a person of that gender. Unless the child has accepted the fact that he is and always will be a boy or a girl, there is no basis for the consistent adoption of sex roles or of sex-typed activities. There is clinical evidence from the case histories of pseudo-hermaphrodites that the gender identity assigned to the child during the first three years of life is crucial for later sex-role development (Hampson, 1965). The social environment normally assigns gender identity to the infant on the basis of the appearance of the external genital organs at birth. But occasionally mistakes are made, as in congenital adrenal hyperplasia, where the internal sexual organs may be female but the external organs are taken as male, especially in infancy. Such individuals typically assume the assigned gender role as children and when the mistake becomes obvious in later childhood they experience considerable difficulty in adjusting to the role which corresponds to their actual gender identity, although most of them eventually appear to do so.

The importance of gender identity was clearly recognized by Freud who assigned great psychological importance to the child's discovery of the differences in the external genitalia of males and females. It is the discovery of the fact that some people have a penis while others do not that is supposed to lead to castration anxiety in boys and penis envy in girls. It is then that the boy identifies with the father and the girl develops the desire to be presented with a penis by its male possessor, that is, to play the receptive feminine sex role.

The trouble with this theory is that it forgets that gender identity is something that exists for the social environment long before it exists for the individual child. We now know that mothers typically treat their male infants and their female infants differently (Moss, 1967) and this lays a basis for sex differences quite apart from the individual's own later recognition of gender identity. Moreover, the adult environment uses the external sex organs of the child as a basis for assigning gender identity long before the child becomes aware of this basis. Research on young children leaves no doubt that they remain unclear about the genital basis of gender identity well after they have clearly accepted their own gender identity. By age four, almost all children are able to assign the correct sex label to themselves and to doll figures they are shown. But the *basis* for their labelling typically involves characteristics like clothing, hair-style and general size. At this age the majority of children are still quite confused about and sometimes ignorant of genital differences. This emerges both in doll-play situations and in a figure-assembly task which involves matching the part containing the genitals with the other parts of the body. Typically, younger children are better at assigning the correct gender identity to clothed than to unclothed figures (Katcher, 1965). It is, therefore, likely that gender identity is first established on other criteria than genital differences, but that the latter eventually become recognized as signifying this identity, as they do for the adult. However, in spite of their common confusion about genital differences, children of four or five already have definite conceptions of sex-role stereotypes and show clear sex-typed differences in behaviour.

An alternative explanation of the formation of gender identity is based on Piaget's work on cognitive development (Kohlberg, 1966). This treats the formation of concepts of gender identity as a specific instance of general conceptual development. The child arrives at the category of gender in the same way as he arrives at other conceptual categories.

by a process of intellectual development which depends on maturation as well as on interaction with the environment.

A child of two does not distinguish clearly between a category and one of its members. It applies the same verbal label indiscriminately to individuals and to classes of individuals. In using a word like 'cat', he would not make the distinction between *this* cat and *any* cat, the difference between class names and proper names being unclear to him. Thus, a label like 'boy' might be used much like a proper name, 'Jim', and the fact that there is more than one individual with the label 'boy' has no more significance than the fact that there is more than one individual with the name 'Jim'. At this stage there is no conception of stable classes and categories distinguished by general criteria. That is why he finds it quite acceptable that a cat might change itself into a dog or a fiddler and a frog into a prince. The stability of species of beings is not established until a later stage of cognitive development and it is only at this later stage that gender identity can be established (Kohlberg and Zigler, 1967), for the formation of gender identity requires the use of sex labels as category labels and not merely as proper names. It requires the formation of general categories whose members are distinguished by certain stable characteristics. It is only when the child is intellectually able to see himself as a member of a class of beings that we can speak of the development of gender identity.

It appears to be a rule for children to show a clear preference for that which is like themselves. Once they have grasped that they are characterized by their membership in a gender category, this colours their evaluation of persons and activities. They become particularly interested in other members of the category and in the qualities that characterize members of that category. It is only then that they begin to show a tendency for preferential identification with adults or older children of the same sex and to apply sex-role standards to their own behaviour. Gender, species and age categories are not mere intellectual divisions for the child who becomes aware of them. They are also moral categories that function as standards rather than simply as cognitive classes. The categories of the animated world have strong 'demand characteristics' for the child at this stage of development – he is innocent of the distinction between fact and value.

From this point of view, the source of the significance of gender identity lies in cognitive development. It is because the first intellectual categories are essentially normative in character that they give the child a set of standards for selecting and accentuating certain stimuli and responses while rejecting others. This is a theory which stresses the role of the internalized selection processes in social development, rather than the role of external socialization pressures.

While there is much to be said for this point of view, it should not lead to a neglect of those factors in the social environment which co-determine the child's adoption of interests and models. Irrespective of any selection imposed by the child's self-categorization, some stimuli are in themselves more appealing than others. Piaget stresses not only the child's tendency to *assimilate* new stimuli to his existing schemata or internalized categories, he also emphasizes the significance of the parallel process of *accommodation* which expresses itself in the child's spontaneous tendency to imitate interesting activities and persons (Piaget, 1951). This process must also be at work in the identification of the child with adults of the same sex. While the formation of gender identity may be a necessary condition for such identification, it is hardly a sufficient condition. If it were, it would scarcely be possible to explain the majority of cases of homosexuality where the individual is in no doubt about his gender identity, nor does he have any desire to change it. Yet, the clinical evidence suggests that such homosexuals identify with parents of the opposite sex (Bieber *et al.*, 1962). If the possibility of there being a constitutional basis for this fairly common situation can be discounted, there must be something about the early social environment of these individuals which leads identification into deviant channels, in spite of the presence of appropriate gender identity and sex-role stereotypes. It is possible that the answer to this question lies in the kind of models which the individual's parents presented.

5 The Parent–Child System

Reciprocity between parent and child

There is one crucial difference between the psychologist who sets himself up as a model to be imitated by his child subjects and the parent who has to cope with his own children. The parent must accommodate to the demands of the child, while the experimenter can afford to ignore them. That is why experiments on imitation yield a very poor simulation of real-life parent–child interaction. The paradigm that equates the parental role with that of the model and the child's role with that of the follower simply does not fit the facts. What mother does not imitate the sounds and smiles of her infant? And who could deny the modelling role of adolescents, at least in respect to dress and speech? In real life the roles are often reversed and it is the child who finds himself in the role of the model or socializing agent to an imitating parent.

If the examples of parental imitation appear marginal, one might ponder the significance of the well-established fact that the same parent will act quite differently with one or other child, or even the same child at different ages. It is difficult to escape the conclusion that the parent accommodates himself to the perceived demands of the child as much as the child accommodates to the demands of the parent. The interaction between them is a two-way process and not one where one partner always represents the active, controlling element and the other partner the passive and malleable element. Children are ingenious at discovering ways of controlling their parents and parents are heavily dependent on their children for all kinds of rewards difficult to obtain outside this relationship.

Perhaps the reason for the long neglect of these truisms by psychological research lies in a widespread bias against admitting the significance of congenital factors among children. A great deal of research on socialization implies a *tabula rasa* conception of the child and the leading role of the adult derives from the fact that he is the source of so much of the experience which becomes engraved on the waxen slate of the child's mind. The analysis of child learning in terms of stimulus and response too often becomes a restatement of the faulty paradigm for which it is always the adult's function to stimulate and the child's function to respond. On the other hand, it is hardly possible to treat the child as the active, controlling partner in the exchange, unless his congenital dispositions are taken into account. There is mounting evidence for congenital differences, at least in respect to restlessness and social responsiveness (Bell, 1968). Some infants are more restless than others and some are less responsive to human stimuli than others and these differences are clearly detectable at a very early stage. Moreover, a number of studies consistently indicate a statistical sex difference, with male infants being somewhat more restless and somewhat less socially responsive. Various non-hereditary factors are known to contribute to increased restlessness or irritability, such as complications of pregnancy and delivery, including effects produced by maternal anxiety.

Now, there is absolutely no doubt that parents are quite sensitive to such differences among infants. In fact, nothing is quite so effective in modifying parental response as variations in the irritability and social responsiveness of the infant. There are studies which illustrate the fact that the same foster mother will show marked differences in her behaviour with different infants and other studies which show that the way in which a mother greets her infant when it is brought to her for feeding is clearly a function of the state of the infant (Levy, 1958). In one case it was demonstrated that the mothers of forty-four sibling pairs were quite inconsistent in the amount of affection given to one or other member of the pair (Lasko, 1954). There is no need to labour the obvious point that the treatment received by the child is not so much an expression of pre-existing parental attitudes but the result of the effect which the child's own propensities have on the parent. Measurement of parent attitudes, therefore, does not enable us to make any predictions, unless we also know something about the child.

A study by Moss (1967) illustrates the reciprocity of the parent–child relation at an early stage of infancy. Using observations of mother–child interaction at the ages of three weeks and three months, Moss demonstrates great changes in the behaviour of both mother and child between the two observation periods. It is not only the child who adapts to the mother's treatment, but also the mother who adapts to changes in the child. This becomes clear when differences in maternal behaviour for male and female infants are examined. Even at three weeks, sex differences in infant behaviour are quite large, especially in terms of the greater irritability of male infants. Apparently, the mother becomes relatively less responsive to the crying of male infants, either because she finds her intervention less effective the greater the infant's irritability or because she has certain fixed ideas about what is to be expected of boys. In any case, these observations suggest that the mother's quietening behaviour may be less dependably evoked by the cry of the male than that of the female infant. But this also means that the mother's response has less influence on the boy's behaviour. In this model of the socialization process, the effectiveness of the 'socializing agent' increases the more his or her behaviour becomes adapted to the requirements of the child. In other words, socialization is seen as a reciprocal relationship in which the control exerted by the 'agent' over the 'target' is itself a function of the control exerted by the 'target' over the 'agent'.

If we take the reality of parent socialization by the child

seriously, we must be prepared to re-examine the implications of past studies which show a correlation between certain parental attitudes and characteristics of their children. Like all correlational studies they leave open the question of the direction of the causal effect, if any. If one abandons the *tabula rasa* bias that became an unquestioned tradition in this area of research, then one must accept the possibility that in some instances differences in parental behaviour have been caused by congenital differences among the children. Some examples will illustrate the point. If children with higher verbal than spatial or numerical ability have a particularly close relationship with their mothers, as one study suggests (Bing, 1963), then we simply cannot conclude that the latter variable is cause, and the former, effect; it is also possible that high-verbal children have a congenitally stronger responsiveness to social stimuli and hence provide their mothers with more reinforcement for interacting with them. Or again, if young boys, found to be more 'masculine' on a test, tend to have fathers who are both highly rewarding and highly punishing, this may simply mean that congenitally more assertive boys please their fathers who then reward them for their 'masculinity' but also have to punish them frequently because their assertiveness creates problems. Correlational studies of parent and child behaviour are always ambiguous in this way.

It is time that we paid more attention to the child's function as a socializing agent, for 'of men and women he makes fathers and mothers' (Rheingold, 1968). Even the young infant has at his disposal two powerful means of controlling his caretakers – the cry and the smile. No wonder the young child believes in the magical power of the human voice and gesture, for his own cry summons powerful beings to his side and his smile first establishes his participation in social life. It is not only the parents who have the power of reward and punishment and the ability to impart information – even a very young infant has a tremendous capacity for rewarding his parents and at least some capacity for informing them of the things that please and displease him. After he has been on the scene for a little while, his parents are not the people they were before – their socialization has begun. It is clear, then, that parent and child form a system in which both partners control and socialize each other and both are dispensers of rewards and sources of information.

The system of mutual demands

In analysing the general characteristics of the interaction between parent and child, one must proceed from the fact that the actions of each partner have a double function for the other. At the beginning, these two functions are sharply separated in the cry and the smile. The infant's cry functions as a demand made on the parent – a demand for caretaking, and the infant's smile functions as a reward or support for the parent, making him feel that his efforts have been worthwhile. Conversely, some of the parent's actions make demands on the child, urging him perhaps to wake up or sit up, or placing restraints on his spontaneous activities. Other actions by the parent nurture and support the child, either physically or, increasingly, psychologically. At the most fundamental level the actions of parents and children towards each other continue to provide demands or supports far beyond the stage of infancy. At the later stages parental demands become oriented to the achievement of socially approved outcomes and the avoidance of disapproved outcomes, while parental support takes a more psychological form. Similarly, the demands made by children change to demands for help with their intellectual and emotional problems, and the reward in store for the parents derives more and more from feelings of pride in their children and emphatic appreciation of childish joys not otherwise available to them.

The demands which parents and children make on each other are of two kinds – positive and negative. Parental demands typically take the form of control behaviour and such controls either set limits on what the child may do or they encourage and stimulate the child to do things he would not otherwise do. The parent either demands that the child desist from an undesirable activity or show more commitment to a desirable activity. Negative demands are involved in parental restriction of the child's 'space of free movement', positive demands involve pressures for the achievement of valued goals. The demands made by the child also take two forms. Firstly, there is the positive demand illustrated by the infant's cry or the older child's clamour for attention. In this case, the child demands some positive form of nurturance from the adult. But there is also the negative demand of the infant who resists being placed in a certain position or the older child who objects to restrictions on his movement or on his choice of food or clothing. Both the child partner and the adult partner in this relationship act so as to keep the other's behaviour within certain favoured limits and they do this by objecting to behaviour above those limits (negative demand or control) or by encouraging behaviour that falls below the required limits (positive demand or control).

It is clear that the mutual demands of parents and children imply a need for mutual support. Every demand is a request for some kind of support (or reinforcement or reward, to use a different language). The positive demands of the parent seek to encourage actions by the child which are rewarding for the parent and negative demands seek to discourage those of the child's action which the parent finds annoying. Similarly, positive demands by the child have the function of increasing nurturing behaviour by the parents and negative demands are meant to reduce the restrictive behaviour of the parents. Each partner in the relationship, therefore, makes demands on the other so as to gain the maximum support from the relationship. As their demands are to some extent incompatible, the final outcome will represent a certain compromise which will depend on their relative effectiveness in pressing their demands.

There is an extensive research literature devoted to the search for the basic dimensions of parental behaviour. While detailed discussion of the methods used will follow later, we may note here that three kinds of data have been used for this purpose: (a) ratings of parental behaviour by observers, as in the Fels Institute studies; (b) measurement of parental attitudes, as undertaken by Schaefer (1959); and (c) cross-cultural studies of parental practices, as illustrated by the work of Minturn and Lambert (1964). While most of these analyses emerge with a bewildering variety of different dimensions, there is a growing consensus among students of the field that two dimensions, in particular, emerge again and again whenever parental behaviour comes under study. These are the dimensions of warmth–hostility on the one hand, and restrictiveness–permissiveness on the other (Becker, 1964). Unfortunately, this field of research has been dominated by profound semantic anarchy and confusion. Every investigator has used his own set of verbal labels for parental characteristics and very often the same term has been used in different ways by different investigators. For instance, the term 'restrictiveness' has been used to refer both to negative and to positive parental demands and sometimes terms like 'dominance' and 'control' are used with the same meaning. In interpreting these studies one must at all costs avoid a kind of verbal realism which takes it for granted that each verbal label refers to a distinct entity in the real world. However, it is possible to say that every relevant study in this field emerges with at least one general dimension of parental control or demand, whatever may be the verbal labels applied to it. In other words, individual differences among parents seem to range themselves along a general dimension of demandingness or permissiveness with some consistency.

When we turn to the other major dimension of parental love or hostility, the limitations of an old-fashioned paradigm for parent–child relations become quite apparent. The actual behaviour which leads to judgements about parental warmth or hostility is necessarily the product of an interaction between parent and child. An instance of parental annoyance may be just as much a function of deliberate provocation on the part of the child as of hostility on the part of the parent. To treat an interaction between two individuals as though the disposition of only one of them contributed to the result is to reduce the other to the status of a passive manipulandum. But in reality the child is anything but passive in his encounters with parents. He presents his demands in no uncertain terms and it is an ideological distortion that traces the outcome of the encounter entirely to the pre-existing attitude of the parent. What the warmth–hostility dimension represents is not a measure of parental attitude but of the success of the parent in meeting the demands of the child. We may assume that a 'warm' atmosphere between parent and child indicates a higher level of demand satisfaction for the child than does a hostile atmosphere. The difference may be due to a difference in the parent, in the child or, more usually, in both; all we really get is a measure of the outcome of their interaction.

The two major dimensions for arranging individual differences in parental behaviour appear to refer to the two most general questions we can ask about these differences. How good is the parent at meeting the child's demands and how demanding is he on the child? There is no need to get bogged down in wrangling over the meaning of terms like 'warmth' and 'permissiveness', for the most relevant features of parental behaviour are simply those that refer to the parent–child relation as a system of mutual demands. If we divide each of our two dimensions down the middle, we get four ideal typical groups of parents: (a) those that are good at satisfying the child's demands and are undemanding themselves; (b) those that are good at satisfying the child's demands but are themselves quite demanding; (c) those that are relatively poor at satisfying the child's demands but are undemanding themselves; and (d) those that are poor at satisfying the child's demands and are quite demanding themselves. It is clear that the same classification could be used for dyadic relationships other than those between parents and children, and there is no reason why this should not be so. It is only from the point of view of the 'waxen tablet' conception of the child that a special set of categories becomes necessary for singling out parent–child relationships among other forms of social interaction. Once it is recognized that the child's role is an active one, the parent–child relationship becomes explicable in terms of quite general categories of social interaction.

Developmental sequence of demands

The demands which individuals make on each other are of three kinds. There are, firstly, pre-verbal demands expressed in a gesture, a cry or a smile. The infant is at first restricted to these, but at a later stage he becomes able to express his demands verbally. For a considerable time the verbal expression of demands is restricted to a statement of preferences in terms of wants and likes as well as aversions and dislikes. Many of the verbal demands of the parent are, of course, on the same level and are simply expressions of preference or evaluation. 'Do this', 'Don't do that', 'This is nice,' 'That is awful,' 'Come here', 'Go away', etc. If such demands are obeyed, it is because of the personal power of the parent, because of his potential ability to enforce them by means of more direct forms of pressure. Similarly, the child's demands may be successful at this level because of his ability to make a nuisance of himself or to make the parent feel sorry for him. There is a big difference between this and the next level where demands typically have to be justified. The older child knows that it is infantile to press one's demand by mere reiteration of one's desire. He tries to justify his demands by an appeal on grounds of fairness, expediency or efficiency and, increasingly, he expects the parent to justify his demands too. The parent who continues to rely solely on expressions of personal preference based on personal power is apt to become less and less effective as the child grows older and learns to respect rules more than he does individuals. The effectiveness of parental demands depends to a large extent on their fit or match with the child's level of development. It is as pointless to appeal to an infant's sense of fairness as it is to deal with an adolescent's complaints by imposing physical restrictions.

To each of the three major stages of imitation or modelling behaviour there corresponds a particular form of social demand. Sensori-motor imitation is a response to a preverbal or gestural demand, identification depends on the communication of verbally expressed evaluations and preferences, and the following of principles indicates the successful justification of demands by appeals to norms and rules. These correspondences are simply an expression of the fundamental truth that *an act of modelling involves an implicit demand.* When a child models the actions of an adult, he is demonstrating the fact that those actions have a distinct 'demand character' for him, whether the adult is aware of this or not. Conversely, a demand directed by a more powerful to a less powerful individual, usually constitutes an actual or potential command, and a command is a verbal representation of something that requires to be modelled. In other words, studies of the modelling process, such as those we have discussed earlier, are in fact studies of the child's reaction to demands emanating from more or less powerful sources. In order to get anything approaching a schematic representation of the situation between parent and child, these studies need to be supplemented by others devoted to the analysis of the child's presentation of his demands. Finally, and most important of all, a theoretical model of the interaction between the two sets of demands is required.

There is one tradition in psychological theory which has attempted to come to grips with this problem. This is the tradition, primarily associated with the writings of Jean Piaget, which traces its origins to the thought of J. M. Baldwin in the early years of this century and finds its most articulate expression in the contemporary work of Lawrence Kohlberg. One important feature of this theoretical orientation is the fundamental distinction of two kinds of relationship between an individual and his environment. In Piaget's terms, this relationship may either take the form of *accommodation*, where the individual alters his own activity in response to an environmental demand, or *assimilation*, where the individual imposes his own activity on the environment. Imitation is the purest example of accommodation, as play is of assimilation. In the one case, the individual is the recipient of environmental demands, in the other case he imposes his own demands on the environment. In imitation the structure of the child's activity is brought closer to the structure presented by the external model; in play, the child's world is structured by the child's intentions. The one attitude is essentially passive, the other essentially active. In the context of parent–child interaction a balance is struck between the child's accommodation to parental demands and his attempts at assimilating the parental figure to the world of his own demands, as when he induces the parent to play a role assigned to him by the child's own fantasy. One might say that in the one case the child rewards the parent by following him, while in the other case the child expects to be rewarded by the parent's following of a scheme initiated by the child.

Many years ago, J. M. Baldwin pointed out that childish imitation of adults was only one side of the coin. The other side was represented by the child's insistence on repeating the acquired performance before an audience. Typically, the act of imitation does not complete a natural sequence of behaviour – it is merely the first step in a two-phase process in which it is followed by a rehearsal of the new act to demonstrate the child's new competence. Without this second phase, imitation remains trivial and has no general or lasting effect on the child's behaviour. Baldwin called the second phase of the process 'ejection', and he used this term in a sense very similar to that of Piaget's use of 'assimilation'. It appears that each of the major developmental stages of imitation involves an analogous stage in the development of 'ejection'. At the sensorimotor stage the child merely seeks to involve the adult in his play; at the stage of identification, the child enacts a role and demands: 'Look at me'; but when he progresses to the modelling of rules rather than of persons this changes to: 'Did I do it right?'

These observations suggest an important difference between behaviour that is reinforced by impersonal rewards, as in many laboratory studies of learning, and behaviour that is reinforced by a successful imitation – ejection sequence. The latter type of learning involves the learner's self-concept, the former does not. In social learning it is not only the source of the reward that is personal, but the outcome has a personal significance too. The learner has become a different person by acquiring some of the actions of another person. Learning to write or to ride a bicycle is not merely a matter of acquiring motor skills, it is also a matter of changing the child's self-concept. Something from a different role repertoire has been added to the child's own repertoire, and he is able to demonstrate to himself and to others that his self is now defined by a different set of roles than before.

The development of a self involves the taking over of the roles and hence the points of view of others. It is a form of sharing. That is why it is misleading to think of socialization as involving the progressive control of a fundamentally asocial individual by social stimuli. There is a sharing of actions through imitation and a mutual satisfaction of demands even during the first year of life. Subsequently, other forms of sharing and reciprocity develop, but it is a case of new forms of social interaction superceding older ones rather than the change of an asocial being into a social one. Socialization is the process which leads to the succession of stages of sharing rather than a process involving the transformation of an aboriginal selfishness. Both self-reward and sharing with others appear very early in the life of the individual; what changes are their forms.

The stages in the development of reciprocity must necessarily be parallel to those already distinguished for imitation–accommodation and ejection–assimilation. At first, reciprocity between self and other is defined in terms of physical reward and punishment. The child will be rewarded or punished for the way in which he carries out parental demands, but conversely the child reciprocates by means of tantrums, crying, etc. if his demands not met. At the stage of identification there is a recognition that positive relationships in the family are based on the reciprocal maintenance of expectations and preferences among the members. This stage is marked by a deliberate attempt at achieving a balance in the distribution of rewards, although this balance reflects the relative power of the different members of the family. At a later stage there develops the conception of a social order as a system of norm-regulated reciprocal rights and duties which extend beyond the parent–child relationship. Thus, at the stage of identification the child will respect a rule because it is a way of rewarding its parent, that is, of fulfilling a parental demand on a reciprocal basis, but at the later stage the rule is seen as binding on both parent and child and is, therefore, respected for its own sake. Parents differ in the degree to which they encourage the transition from the one stage to the other and many individuals never develop a strong commitment to the more abstract forms of reciprocity.

6 Personality Formation in the Family

It is time to return from the somewhat abstract excursions of the previous chapter to the kinds of concerns that lead to the study of socialization in the first place. In the earlier sections of this volume we noted that these concerns arose out of certain very real social problems. We established that these problems did not yield particularly viable concepts for objective research and we suggested that an approach via more abstract, 'geno-typical' concepts was indicated. Now, while research on imitation and the patterns of parent–child interaction may have some intrinsic interest, its relevance to important human problems remains an open question. Moreover, the world does not stop while we pursue the slow process of empirical research and conceptual analysis with its multitude of unavoidable blind alleys. People continue to plague themselves and others with their personality problems and they demand answers to questions that do not permit shelving. As long as we maintain our faith in the proposition that childhood experience plays *some* role in personality formation we cannot avoid confronting the possible relationships between parent–child interaction and the development of the individual's personality, both in its desired and its undesired aspects.

It is perfectly natural that a large speculative literature should have grown up around this issue. People demand a framework for interpreting themselves to themselves, especially in time of crisis; and as the complexities of the human situation are almost infinite, no idea, no matter how far-fetched, need ever die for lack of concrete illustration by means of 'case material' or whatever. Without involving ourselves in the philosophical question of the precise status of such ideas, it is quite clear that their truth value is quite different from that of 'scientific' theories which are expressed in terms that make their disconfirmation possible, at least in principle. Not that general concepts are ever directly confirmed or disconfirmed by observation and experiment. But we do have to distinguish between those general concepts from which we might deduce specific hypotheses subject to potential disconfirmation and other general concepts which do not lend themselves to this procedure. In the present volume we have tried to restrict ourselves to the former type of concept, though we shall continue to be fairly liberal in accepting claims to potential empirical disconfirmation, accepting the risk that future analysis and research may show some of these claims to have been false. In the present chapter we shall stretch this liberality to its limit rather than accept defeat in the face of the evident chasm between what has so far been accomplished by empirical research and the magnitude of the questions that remain unanswered.

Cognitive style

That the quality of intellectual interest and functioning may be influenced by parental behaviour is not a particularly recent notion. James Mill, in the belief that a man's character and intellect could be completely determined by his education, tutored his young son himself. John Stuart Mill became a remarkable prodigy, working diligently under the strict supervision of his father. The young Mill was isolated from his peers, sharing a study with his father. At their table, side by side, they pursued their academic tasks. Before John Stuart Mill was eight years old, he displayed a considerable knowledge of Latin and Greek. By the age of twelve he had read through a vast quantity of classical literature. Under his father's stern tutelage, coupled with the example of assiduous dedication to learning, the boy grew up believing his achievements to be nothing out of the ordinary. Apparently James Mill not only failed to indicate to his son that other young boys led different lives, but also conveyed that John's achievements were not quite as accomplished as those of his peers. The biographies of musical prodigies provide further examples of young children who had their noses held to the grindstone by parents intent on perfecting the skills of their offspring. One of the most notable was the young Beethoven who was subjected to fierce bullying by a tyrannical father.

For some time the concept of intelligence, as expressed in scores achieved on psychometric tests, was taken as the major indicator of cognitive functioning. Numerous studies attempted to weigh the effects of genetic or environmental factors on the I Q level of the child, frequently by making comparisons between identical twins reared apart. The results have been equivocal, with supporters of both positions using the same evidence to argue their own point equally strongly. Longitudinal studies concerned with changes in I Q scores – cumulative increments or losses – have been somewhat more interesting. Children growing up in culturally deprived environments have shown a steady decline in tested I Q scores. One longitudinal study showed that a group of children who progressively increased their I Q scores over a number of years had parents who were described as warm and supporting by the researchers and allowed their children a great deal of freedom in exploring their environment. A twenty-eight-year longitudinal investigation begun in the late 1920s (Honzik, 1967) found that some aspects of parental behaviour were associated with optimal cognitive and mental development. The boys in this study appeared to need an initially warm and close relationship with their mother in the early years, followed in adolescence by a lessening of attachment to her. A friendly, but not necessarily affectionate, relationship with the father fostered optimal cognitive growth in the girls. While these observations are interesting, no generalizations should be based on the results of a single study.

As conventional intelligence tests provide merely a measure of a product or yield, they need to be supplemented by more process-oriented tests if the socialization of cognitive functioning is to be further analysed. In particular, qualitative differences in mode of intellectual functioning need to be looked at. One feature of intelligent behaviour is the way in which the world is organized and subsequently interpreted. Some people may employ only a limited number of categories for organizing information about their world, not because basic intellectual ability is lacking, but because this is the preferred mode of interacting with a disturbingly complex environment. Personality factors, or preferred modes of approaching the world, play as strong a part here as the level of intelligence.

Two preferred modes of approach to complex problems have been termed 'field independent' and 'field dependent'. The field independent person performs in a superior manner on any task where an embedding context needs to be overcome. In the field independent approach, the object is kept separate from the surrounding field; this has also been labelled an 'analytical' cognitive style. The field dependent approach, in which object and field tend to fuse, has been described as 'global'. Such cognitive styles, whether global or analytical, extend not only to a wide variety of intellectual tasks, but are also associated with certain personality characteristics. One of the personality features which characterize the field independent person is a clearly defined sense of separate identity, which emerges in testing situations. There is greater involvement in the task with less reassurance seeking from outside sources. Another characteristic is a greater ability to articulate personal experience in a discrete and structured way, without losing the inter-relationships between events. In answer to questions about experiencing the everyday life situation ('Tell me a bit about yourself', 'What is your mother like?'), field independent children reveal a greater degree of cognitive clarity, displaying a clear and organized experience of self and the world. Other associated features are a greater tolerance for complexity and ambiguity, and a greater flexibility in changing set when a particular problem-solving approach fails in producing a solution.

There are strong indications that degree of field independence is associated with different child-rearing practices. Similarities between the child's and his mother's cognitive style have often been reported. There is also a suggestion that field independent mothers respond more differentially to the infant's crying, interpreting the quality of his cry as expressing different demands. Field dependent mothers follow a general policy of attending to the infant's cry or not, without making finer distinctions. Presumably such differential interpretation of an infant's demands reinforces a reciprocal pattern of greater differentiation in the infant's response. Male infants, on the whole, are more restless and cry more than girl infants. Boys also tend to do better on tests measuring field independence than girls do. There is a possibility that the behaviour of the male infant demands a more differentiated response on the part of the mother. This woud lead to differences in patterns of interaction between mother and child, depending on the sex of the infant.

In contrast to this the verbal superiority of girls on tasks reflecting linguistic facility, is frequently noted. Here, too, the mother's pattern of communication may play a role. Several studies have pointed to the fact that mothers talk more to their daughters than to their sons, even in infancy. One study explored the relationship between the mother's level of verbal stimulation and children's scores on verbal tests (Bing, 1963). The children had similar total IQ scores, but were divided by sex into 'high' and 'low' verbal groups, based upon the contrast of verbal with spatial and numerical scores. Results indicated that a higher level of verbal stimulation from the mother was an especially significant factor in affecting the verbal score of boys. Another important finding – also especially significant in the case of boys – was the fact that these mothers reported remembering more of the child's early accomplishments. This may reflect the mother's greater verbal ability to articulate events as much as the accuracy of her memory, suggesting similarities between the mother and child's level of linguistic competence.

Recent research shows a greater concern with the investigation of parent–child interaction and its relationship with the development of specific cognitive skills. This direction promises to go beyond vague concepts of 'enriched experience' and 'general intelligence', and to show more clearly the processes by which parental behaviour influences or modifies cognitive development.

Beyond the parent–child dyad

It has been pointed out that at the most abstract level the parent's influence on the child depends on two sets of factors: (a) the demands he presents to the child, including the implicit demands of the model to be imitated, and (b) his success in satisfying the child's demands. Now, it is immediately obvious that the parent's effectiveness in either of these directions will be limited by a host of extraneous circumstances which determine the time and the resources at the disposal of the parent. For example, the relative material poverty of the parent makes it difficult or impossible to provide certain kinds of support for the child's demands and will be likely to lead to a heavier reliance on nonmaterial rewards. Again, the number of children that have to be taken care of, relative to the time that adult caretakers can potentially contribute, will make a difference to the way in which demands are presented. If caretaking time is in short supply, patience goes overboard and demands must be presented in a relatively peremptory manner. It is hardly surprising to find that, irrespective of social class, parents of larger families are more likely to be seen as autocratic by their children and as not explaining the rules they imposed than parents of smaller families (Elder and Bowerman, 1963).

The type and level of parental demands and supports, as well as the manner in which they are presented to the child, are also limited by cultural and subcultural norms and rules, a topic that will be considered in chapters 10 and 11.

At this point it is appropriate to remind ourselves that most of the discussion of the previous chapters was based on a temporarily convenient fiction, the fiction of the isolated parent—child dyad. Of course, socialization is not an affair involving only two individuals, adult and child, model and learner, etc. In real life, third parties are generally involved, whether in the shape of the other parent, siblings, grandparents or other relatives. The effect of the individual parent's influence will, therefore, be mediated by a complex pattern of family relationships. The mere presence of additional models may be significant. Thus, one study reports that at the pre-school level, the presence of an older brother promotes more 'masculine' behaviour and the presence of an older sister promotes more 'feminine' behaviour in boys (Brim, 1958).

But the crucial factor lies in the fact that for most families triangular, rather than dyadic, interaction forms the simplest molecule to which our analysis can be reduced. In chapter 3 we stressed the significance of the power position of the adult who is to become the child's model. We suggested that the ease with which an adult was adopted as a model by the child would depend to a significant degree on the relative power which the adult was judged to have in a social system that the child was in a position to observe. The family is, of course, the first such system to which the child is normally exposed. What he sees of the interaction of his parents will make him favour one or other of them as a model for identification. If the dominant parent is also of the same sex as the child and if his dominance is in line with sex-role stereotypes, all salient factors seem to work in the same direction. Thus, it is not surprising to find considerable convergence among studies of boys' masculine role identification. In families where the father is seen as dominant there is a greater tendency for boys to show a preference for the male role and to display personality characteristics that are similar to those of the father (Hetherington, 1965). But maternal dominance appears to be a source of stress for boys because the tendency to adopt the dominant parent as a model must lead to conflicts about sex role and personal identity. While studies in this area are not often well designed, it is difficult to deny the weight of a mass of convergent evidence on this question. At least certain types of male schizophrenics, for example, appear to have this kind of family background (Fleck, Lidz and Cornelison, 1963).

It is hardly necessary to stress that what the child sees of the behaviour of his parents to each other will help to determine the *content* of what he models or imitates, quite apart from the question of which parent is preferentially imitated. The *consistency* of the demands made on the child by mother and father will also play a role. Ideally there should be a match between the pattern presented by the dominant-role model and the reciprocal or complementary role expectations of the other partner. But where there is serious dissension and lack of complementarity between mother and father, the child is presented with conflicting demands. Not being able to satisfy both sets of demands satisfactorily, the child is left with a feeling of inadequacy and self-doubt. Indeed, on the basis of studies of the effects of marital-role tensions on children, Farber (1962) has suggested that 'the child's sense of self-worth may be more a function of the quality of the husband–wife interaction system than the parent–child system'.

The presence of siblings introduces a further complication in that the parent now has to make demands on and give support to more than one child. The fact that siblings provide an audience for the interaction of any particular parent–child dyad will modify that interaction and its effects for both parents and child. Siblings, especially if they are relatively close together in age, provide a *comparison level* for each other which determines the way each will assess the demands and rewards issuing from the parents. The impact of parental demands and acts of support never has an absolute value but depends on what the child has come to regard as appropriate in any particular context (Kagan, 1967). The child of a generally demanding parent develops a different standard for the severity of parental demands than the child of a relatively undemanding parent. Thus 'strict' parents are often able to continue successfully making much heavier demands on the child than parents who have been more lax in the past. A similar relativity prevails in respect to acts of parental support. A single act of warmth or generosity on the part of a generally stern father will evoke a much greater reaction than one from a generally easy-going father.

However, the standard against which individual parental acts are judged does not depend only on the history of the child's own experience, it also depends on how the parent's behaviour towards the child's siblings is perceived. The same parental demand will be judged quite differently if the sibling is exposed to the same level of demand than if he is not. Because of his cognitive immaturity the child may apply quite unrealistic standards of abstract equality which often leave him with a feeling that unreasonable demands are being made on him and that a younger sibling is being favoured. He finds it difficult to make allowances for age and situational differences, and his expectation of appropriate levels of support for himself are still based on a standard formed before the younger sibling arrived on the scene. He may then try to even things out by making additional demands for attention, a manoeuvre which generally leads to the vicious circles of sibling rivalry which colour the child's interaction with his parents and which may have consequences for his personality development.

But apart from the child's contribution to this situation, genuine parental favouritism also operates. In actual fact, few parents equalize the levels of demand and support for all their children and the child's perception of inequality of treatment may have perfectly good grounds. It is difficult to escape the conclusion that such situations will have repercussions on the child's self-concept. If the child models what he perceives to be the parent's differential assessment of his worth, this may lead to self-doubt in the one case and to 'narcissistic' overvaluation in the other. After that, internal personality dynamics take over and the one attitude may act as a defence against the other.

Family norms

It is clear that the interaction of family members forms a social system whose parts mutually influence each other. Such a system of interacting parts can only persist over a considerable period of time if it is equipped with regulatory devices that maintain the boundaries of the system as a whole and the boundaries of each contributing section. In social systems such regulating devices are provided by norms or rules of behaviour which prescribe the limits of appropriate action for the participants. Like other social systems, families tend to develop norms of right and proper behaviour which are partly idiosyncratic and partly reflections of general cultural norms. These norms assign to each family member an appropriate set of activities, promoting complementarity in the behaviour of each member towards each other member. Such norms regulate the interaction of individuals, setting limits for demands that may legitimately be made. Acts of support frequently function to reinforce normatively required behaviour and their withholding serves to inhibit prescribed behaviour. The exchange of demand and support among family members, therefore, displays more stability over time than it would do if it depended only on the momentary whims of the individuals concerned. Such norms do not require explicit verbal expression to be effective; many instances of social interaction include an implicit or non-verbally expressed appeal to norms.

Because family members commonly give or withhold

support from each other in a pattern that reinforces family norms, the satisfaction of the pre-adolescent child's demands pretty well depends on his acceptance of these norms. They are, therefore, extremely effective in modifying the behaviour of the child, even when the behaviour demanded appears most unfortunate to an outside observer. There are clinically well-authenticated cases of children's collusion in playing the role of family scapegoat assigned to them by norms, protecting the family as a whole from stresses that would prove disastrous to all its members. Such mechanisms may well suppress the type of comparison process described above, because the scapegoat is made to feel that his nature and status are such that comparison with others would be inappropriate. The consequences for personality development are likely to prove all the more disastrous.

The normative assignment of different family roles is not limited to pathological cases. Parents naturally vary their role prescriptions with the age and sex of the child and often with birth order. Thus, first-born children are likely to have somewhat heavier demands placed on them at home and to accept the responsibility imposed by these demands. Hence they show some tendency to do better at adult-approved activities, like schoolwork, and this perhaps predisposes them to excel in intellectual pursuits later on (Clausen, 1966). The fact that they also have relatively more interaction with adults than later-born children is presumably also relevant, as there may be an effect on certain aspects of cognitive development. First born and only children engage less in non-social speech patterns than later-born children (Rubin, Hultsch and Peters, 1971). Because the first-born child is also likely to experience a sudden reduction in the amount of attention and affection accorded to him, he is more likely to experience conflict over the issue of dependence and independence. Hence he is more likely to seek and to benefit from the company of others when he is anxious and at the same time he is less likely to be rated as sociable and outgoing (Sampson, 1965).

Research on the effects of family norms has barely scratched the surface of a vast and complex area. Some significant questions have been raised by psychiatrists interested in the study of families with schizophrenic children. The rigidity and inflexibility of role demands placed on the child may be one factor that plays a role in precipitating a psychotic reaction (Wynne, Ryckoff, Day and Hirsch, 1958). Another possible pathogenic pattern is one in which family members deny that any of them are in fact setting family norms, thus leading to peculiar difficulties in communication (Haley, 1959). Or, again, the parent may simultaneously imply opposed sets of norms in one and the same communication addressed to the child (Bateson, Jackson, Haley and Weakland, 1956). Such a pattern may make it difficult for the child to develop a coherent self-concept.

Socialization and ego development

The various aspects of family functioning need to be taken into account in any attempt to assess the significance of particular patterns of parental demands and supports for the child's personality development. Apart from some consensus about the fact that fathers who make severe negative demands are likely to inhibit ambition and creativity in their sons, there is little convincing or consistent evidence to report in this field. The point is, of course, that the effects of severity of parental demands are not only mediated by a host of other factors, but that the notion of 'severity' itself is relative. The reports of outside observers have little to do with how the child itself experiences this 'severity', because two different standards of comparison are operating. The middle-class professional observer either uses special subcultural norms or statistical standards as a basis for comparison. However, neither of these is known to the child, who has only his own experience to go on. Provided the level of parental severity is reasonably consistent, so that the child can build up a stable internalized comparison level, very high levels of severity may be tolerated with relative equanimity, at least until the child is exposed to discrepant standards outside the home. The crucial effect lies in the establishment of the internalized standard as such, for this will determine the individual's response to various pressures to which he might be exposed as an adult.

The notion of 'optimal level' has been used by Bronfenbrenner (1958a) to draw similar conclusions for the operation of parental support. The child who has become accustomed to a high level of parental affection and reward is more sentive to its absence than the child who has learned to live with less of these things. The consequence is that the former is more sensitive to the withdrawal of support and more readily reacts with compliance to this threat. To ensure the same degree of compliance, much harsher treatment would have to be meted out to the child that does not expect high levels of support. In each case there is a different optimal level of demands for ensuring compliance. The child accustomed to strong support is more vulnerable to the threat of 'oversocialization' in the sense of overcompliance with externally imposed demands; the child with a lower internalized comparison level for support is more vulnerable to the threat of irresponsibility. Bronfenbrenner suggests that this kind of model may help to explain the different reactions of boys and girls to social pressure.

It must be emphasized that the effects of the level of demand and support interact strongly and cannot be considered in isolation from each other. A pertinent distinction is that made by Baumrind (1966) between 'authoritarian' and 'authoritative' homes. Both are characterized by high levels of control, but in the former this is accompanied by lack of warmth and support, while in the latter, severe demands are balanced by effective levels of support. While authoritarian parents tend to have children with high levels of displaced aggression and an externalized conscience, the children of authoritative parents are more likely to be rated as 'mature' and 'stable' by observers. It does not appear fruitful to investigate the effects of child-rearing variables in isolation as interaction effects are likely to be quite crucial determining outcomes.

At times, these interaction effects can be conveniently analysed in terms of so-called 'moderator variables' (Kogan and Wallach, 1964) which are identifiable factors that affect the empirical relationship between two variables. For instance, a certain pair of socialization and personality variables may be found to be correlated for males but not for females; in that case sex functions as a 'moderator variable'. One area in which the relationships between parent and child behaviour have been demonstrated to depend heavily on such 'moderator variables' is the area of aggressiveness in both parents and children. While it is generally true that parents who use severe physical punishment and/or show little warmth and affection have markedly aggressive children (Feshbach, 1970), there are a number of factors which complicate the issue, including the sex and social status of the parent and the sex and age of the child. For instance, maternal restrictiveness with older boys is associated with higher levels of aggression but this does not hold for young boys or for girls (Kagan and Moss, 1962). The effects of paternal punishment, on the other hand, depend on occupational level; punitive high-status fathers appear to be much more likely to have aggressive sons than punitive low-status fathers (Eron, Walder, Toigo and Lefkowitz, 1963).

It must be emphasized that parental firmness and parental warmth and support for the child are quite different dimensions of behaviour, and that any set of parents may well receive a high score on both these scales. Indeed, it appears to be precisely such parents that are most likely to have children characterized by high self-esteem. An important study by Coopersmith (1967) has shown that the optimum conditions for the development of high self-esteem in children involve a combination of firm enforcement of limits on the child's behaviour, together with a large degree of acceptance of the child's autonomy within those limits. Provided these parentally imposed limits are reinforced by social norms outside the family, this leads the child to a definition of an orderly and trustworthy social reality which provides a firm basis for his own actions. Although the parents of such children were not only more demanding in a negative, limit-setting sense, but also made stronger positive demands for achievement, their simultaneous support of the child's limited autonomy provided a favourable soil for the development of a positive self-concept.

It is tempting to contrast these findings with the results of some of the more carefully designed studies of the interaction between parents and their schizophrenic children (Lennard, Beaulieu and Embrey, 1965; Mishler and Waxler, 1968). One convergent set of findings from this area focuses on the rather consistent tendency of these parents to deny communicative support to the schizophrenic child. They often do not respond to the child's statements and demands for a recognition of his own point of view; their own communications are often intrusions and interventions rather than replies to the child. In fact, they respond selectively to those of the child's expressions which have been initiated by themselves rather than to any expressions initiated by the child. It is as though he were being denied the right to autonomy. At the same time, interaction proceeds in a rather stereotyped manner which sets such narrow limits on spontaneous expression as to render it practically impossible.

One may speculate that the primary effect of patterns of parental demand and support lies in the establishment of ego boundaries, that is, in the creation of a zone of self-expression bounded by a clearly perceived social reality. In the absence of such boundaries there is confusion between self and non-self; impaired appreciation of external reality and impaired autonomy of the self are mutually complementary (Laing, 1961). The development of effective ego boundaries depends on both the demands and the supports for which socialization agents are the source. A boundary is, of course, a relationship. To establish the kind of relationship between 'inside' and 'outside' which we associate with normal personality functioning, parental demands must establish wide but firm limits within which generous support is extended to the growth of autonomous ego functions.

Any attempt to search for the relationships between personality development and family life must ultimately come to grips with the fact that there is an element of discontinuity in child development. That is to say, that there are qualitatively distinct levels of social interaction, and in the life of the child these levels emerge gradually in some kind of epigenetic sequence. For Freud these levels were represented by the stages of psychosexual development. In spite of the allegorical form of his account, its considerable appeal was partly based on the fact that it did, at least, provide a basis for a reconstruction of personality development that recognized the importance of different functional levels. More recently, Piaget has given an account of the stages of cognitive development which has found its way into general psychology and which has proved fruitful for much empirical research. The stages of social learning distinguished in chapters 3 and 5 owe much to this approach.

In the last section of chapter 5 it was pointed out that to each stage of development there corresponded a particular form of social demand. The earliest demands to which the child can respond, and which he is capable of making himself, are pre-verbal or gestural. This is followed by the verbal expression of preferences or desires at the second stage and by the appeal to norms and rules at the third stage. It is obvious that a similar distinction can be made for the different kinds of support that the child demands and receives from his parents. At the earliest stage this support is essentially physical, linked to the satisfaction of primary needs, including needs for physical contact and environmental stability. Thereafter, the child requires support in his exploration of the physical and social environment through the manipulation of objects and the playing of roles. Finally, the child looks for support in his attempts at following rules and doing things right. One might say that the demands for parental support which the child makes are demands for *recognition* or *confirmation* as a certain kind of being. At first the child needs to be recognized as a dependent creature in need of comfort and contact. Later he wants to be recognized as a doer, he wants to be looked at and to have his real or imagined achievements confirmed by an audience. Finally, he asks to be confirmed as a *good* creature who does things right and who knows the rules.

Personality development can be looked at as the achievement of some balance between the individual's need to make demands on others and his ability to recognize the demands which others make on him. A gross lack of balance in either direction will lead to unsatisfactory social relationships. In the one case, he overwhelms others with his demands, in the other case, he overwhelms himself by subjectively distorting and exaggerating the demands which others make on him. Quite commonly, of course, this lack of balance expresses itself in erratic swings from one extreme to the other. This description is quite analogous to that which Piaget uses to characterize cognitive development. The common conception lies in the recognition of the interplay between assimilatory and accomodatory mechanisms (Piaget, 1951). As was mentioned at the end of the last chapter, the latter ultimately refers to an alteration of the individual in favour of an environmental demand, while the former refers to the individual's imposition of his own demands on the environment. Personality development, no less than intellectual development, involves the achievement of a balance between these two poles. In other words, personality development involves the unfolding of satisfactory levels of reciprocity between ego and alter.

The achievement of this balance may be considered to depend on the balance and consistency of demands and supports which the individual has been exposed to at various stages of his development. Gross imbalance or inconsistency in the externally presented demand–support structure is unlikely to be conducive to the achievement of a balanced internal structure. However, in view of the qualitative difference between stages of development, such inadequacies may be more marked for one level of functioning than for others. This would depend on the particular strengths and weaknesses of the child's socialization agents. Their task is not an easy one. Some parents may find it difficult to extend recognition and support to the child's demands on *any* level – the studies of the families of some schizophrenics seem to suggest this. Other parents may find it difficult to match their support with the level of demand presented by the young child. For example, a rigid insistence on treating the child as a rule-following creature at a stage when it is merely his basic dependency that needs to be recognized may make it difficult for him to solve the problems of either stage.

In the clinically oriented literature on personality development, it is particularly the work of E. H. Erikson (1950) that has attracted the attention of students of socialization. Erikson was among the first to draw attention to the fact that the stages of early personality development had to be regarded as stages in the development of patterns of mutuality or reciprocity between ego and alter, and that at each stage a conflict between opposite poles of this relationship had to be resolved. So we get the successive crises to which he applied the clinically convenient labels of 'trust–distrust', 'confidence–doubt' and 'initiative–guilt'. This represented a transition from the highly allegorical body language of the orthodox psychoanalyst to the kinds of terms that lend themselves, at least potentially, to social psychological investigation. Just as Piaget linked the common terms 'play' and 'imitation' to cognitive behaviour marked by lack of balance between assimilatory and accommodatory processes, so it may be possible to understand Erikson's polar pairs as involving a similar lack of balance in the development of social reciprocity. At each stage of development this conflict assumes qualitatively different forms for which Erikson's terms supply intuitively meaningful labels. It is over conceptual bridges such as these that the dialogue between experimentalists and clinicians may be productively resumed without the virtues of either approach being lost in the process.

7 Moral Development

The study of social conditions affecting the child's moral development has been marked by clearly divergent conceptions of the nature of moral development. Different studies of moral development do not necessarily share the same understanding of the phenomenon that is to be explained. In fact, a clear separation has developed between three distinct conceptions of moral development, depending on which of the three basic psychological levels – behaviour, affect and judgement – are considered to define the essence of morality.

For some, studying moral development is essentially a matter of studying certain aspects of *behaviour*, namely, the overt response or lack of response to conventional social demands. For this orientation, the favourite technique of assessing moral development has been the measurement of resistance to the temptation to transgress recognized social rules about such matters as cheating, telling lies, etc. If the individual does not transgress these rules, in the absence of external sanctions, some evidence for the internalization of moral prescriptions appears to have been obtained. It is then possible to study the antecedents of greater or lesser degrees of resistance to temptation.

The classical study representing this approach is found in the famous work by Hartshorne and May (1928–30). In extensive tests of resistance to temptation under a variety of conditions, they found that for pre-adolescents there was very little correlation between dishonesty and cheating in different types of situation. If a child cheats in one situation we can for all practical purposes say nothing about the likelihood of his cheating in a different type of situation.

Moreover, children were not clearly divisible into an 'honest' and a 'dishonest' group – most of them being moderately honest. It also became clear that the tendency to cheat depended in large measure on the perceived risk of detection, so that non-cheaters were probably more cautious rather than more honest. There is thus considerable doubt about the very existence of a general factor in the development of moral behaviour, although a more recent re-analysis of the Hartshorne and May data has indicated that there is a general factor involved in various instances of cheating in a classroom situation (Burton, 1963).

Subsequent work on the strictly behavioural aspects of moral development has confirmed the overwhelming importance of situational factors. Moreover, there is no evidence that 'resistance to temptation' is a personality characteristic with longitudinal stability. A child's 'honesty' at one age does not appear to have any value for predicting his ability to resist temptation at a later age.

In the light of these findings it has often seemed appropriate to regard moral behaviour as due to specific habits rather than as an expression of general moral character. These habits would be acquired as a result of the pattern of rewards and punishments meted out by the agents of socialization in particular situations. It is not surprising to find that attempts to relate global assessments of parental child-rearing patterns to children's moral behaviour have yielded quite inconsistent results. Some studies have reported positive relationships between parental nurturance and resistance to temptation, but others have not (Kohlberg, 1963b). Extremely hostile and rejecting parents are more likely to have delinquent children, but within the normal range the value of a given reward or punishment depends on its relation to the overall level of nurturance. The same effective reward and punishment can, therefore, occur under quite different overall conditions of nurturance. Behavioural conformity to specific norms in particular situations is more likely to depend on situation-specific sanctions than on the general pattern of parent–child relationships. In the light of all these considerations it must be seriously doubted whether the use of 'resistance to temptation' measures offers much promise of increasing our understanding of the antecedents of moral development.

Many students of moral development have preferred to use the occurrence of guilt reactions in response to transgression as a criterion of moral development. This appears to avoid the problems caused by the operation of morally irrelevant factors in the 'resistance to temptation' situation. It is possible to yield to temptation and yet to show one's sensitivity to moral standards by a guilt reaction.

While this approach to the study of moral development owes something to psychoanalytic theories, its implications are in fact opposed to Freud's essential contributions to the study of the human conscience. The central propositions of that contribution were concerned with the destructive effects (both on the individual and the social level) of an unconscious guilt whose severity had very little relationship to external factors, either in childhood or in later life. Freud always emphasized the price paid by the individual for the privileges of social life. Ignoring these themes, American learning theorists like Mowrer preferred to regard guilt as an acquired anxiety reaction to the anticipation of physical pain or loss of love. This anxiety protects the individual from the consequences of anti-social actions he might otherwise indulge in. There is no distinction between non-conformity and immorality, nor is there any real distinction between the acquisition of conditioned fear responses and the acquisition of internalized symbolic standards for behaviour. Neither Freud's nor Mowrer's views have had much influence on contemporary research in this area.

Two measures of guilt have often been used: 'confession', and self-blame or self-criticism. In these studies the child is commonly exposed to an incomplete story in which the central character transgresses a moral rule and the child has to indicate what happens afterwards. One can then see to what extent the child attributes responses like self-blame and confession to the story character after his transgression. These confession responses must be regarded as specific instrumental responses to obtain parental forgiveness. They are related to the child's dependency on the parents rather than to his moral development and their use by the child depends on the parent's manipulation of the dependency relationship for the purpose of obtaining compliance. This happens when the parent uses 'love withdrawal' as a technique for expressing disapproval and makes the expression of affection contingent on the child's good behaviour.

Self-critical responses appear to have different antecedents to confession responses and are not correlated with them. Unlike confession, self-criticism has more than an instrumental, approval-seeking function. A number of studies have shown a positive relationship between self-critical responses and resistance to temptation and non-delinquency (Allinsmith, 1960). There is also a clearer development of these responses with age than is the case for confessional responses. Self-critical responses are not necessarily addressed to an external audience, like a confession, and their function seems to be more related to internalized control over one's behaviour than to attempts at restoring social approval.

In the older child-training literature it was customary to make a distinction between 'psychological' techniques of discipline, which included the expression of verbal disapproval, reasoning and explaining, and more direct forms of discipline, including physical punishment and verbal assault. While the distinction was not usually made with great precision and while its exact connotations differed from one writer to another, all the relevant studies appear to agree in showing the superiority of 'psychological' techniques in producing higher levels of self-control in the child. This may, of course, be due to the fact that parents using 'psychological' techniques are almost certain to be more self-controlled than parents using direct techniques and in each case the child simply imitates the model of behaviour presented to him by the parent.

Aronfreed (1961) has pointed out that what direct methods of discipline have in common is that they sensitize the child to the anticipation of punishment; they reinforce the child for attention to the potential punitive responses of others. On the other hand, 'psychological' types of discipline expand the child's own cognitive resources for internalized control of its own behaviour by focusing attention on his intentions and on general principles of conduct. In other words, the child's control of its own behaviour becomes less dependent on external contingencies and more dependent on its own cognitive resources. Aronfreed uses the terms 'sensitization' and 'induction' to refer respectively to direct and 'psychological' techniques of discipline, and this usage appears to have some advantages over the older terminology. It is not surprising to find considerable agreement among a number of studies, showing a fairly consistent positive relationship between parental use of inductive methods of discipline and the child's use of self-critical responses to transgression. Such responses would, of course, be fostered by parental efforts at getting the child to react to the general implications and the intentions involved in his actions, which is the essence of inductive methods of discipline.

On a more general level, it is possible to see sensitization as being essentially a sensitization to parental demands, while induction involves the support of the child by supplying the cognitive resources which he requires for monitoring his own behaviour. The findings just reported suggest that the development of strong internalized standards of conduct may depend on the parental demand–support ratio. Unfortunately, studies in this area have not effectively distinguished between cognitive and emotional demands and supports. The two may be independent. It is possible for the same parent to be emotionally demanding and cognitively supportive or vice versa. Perhaps this accounts for the poor relationship that exists between moral principles and moral conduct. An individual who has received strong cognitive support may well develop high moral principles and strong self-critical reactions, but his actual conduct may fall far short of these prescriptions. The translation of moral principles into possibly unpopular actions is likely to be related to such factors as the degree of self-acceptance of the individual, which will depend on the emotional rather than on the cognitive support he has received.

In order to trace the socialization process involved in moral development it is necessary to distinguish not only between moral behaviour and moral standards, but also between responses meant to obtain or restore social approval and moral responses as such. This distinction has already been referred to in connection with the difference between confession reactions and self-critical reactions in response to transgression. The former, like restitution reactions, belong to a broad class of instrumental actions designed to placate powerful social figures and need not imply any internalized moral standards at all. They are fostered, as we have noted, by parental use of love-withdrawal techniques of discipline which teach the child that compliance to social norms is the price of parental love. On the other hand, the development of self-critical reactions without overt social compliance does not seem to depend on the experience of contingent love so much as on the induction of remorse by reasoning, pointing out the harm done to others, etc. (Hoffman, 1969). Such techniques involve the direct stimulation of the child's capacity for moral self-judgement rather than the production of guilt by punishment.

It has, therefore, seemed appropriate to some students of this area to look at moral development essentially in terms of cognitive, judgemental processes, rather than in terms of behaviour or of affective guilt reactions. It is true that moral judgements play *some* role in 'resistance to temptation' but, as we have seen, their role is usually eclipsed by purely situational factors, assessment of risk, etc. Moral judgements are also involved in guilt reactions, but here it is often impossible to disentangle their effect from the frequently more powerful motive of social compliance and the restoration of social approval. If we wish to raise questions about the socialization processes involved in the genesis of moral judgements as such, we have to study them directly and not in their entanglement with situational contingencies or extraneous approval motives.

This approach goes back to Jean Piaget's classic study on *The Moral Judgement of the Child* (1932). Piaget asked children between the ages of four and thirteen to judge the 'naughtiness' of the actions of various story characters, to assess the appropriateness of punishments in different kinds of situation, to comment on the fairness of divisions of responsibility in a number of hypothetical cases, and so on. On the basis of the children's replies he concluded that certain aspects of moral judgement were subject to clear age differences which seemed to indicate a developmental sequence. Among these differences the following are of special importance: young children differ from older children in judging an act as bad in terms of its physical consequences rather than in terms of the intention behind it; they are unaware of relativism in moral judgement and do not admit any diversity of views about right and wrong; they regard an act as bad because it will be punished, not because it breaks a rule, harms others, etc.; and finally, young children do not use reciprocity as a reason for consideration of others. Piaget described many other aspects of age-related changes in moral judgement, but their generality is in doubt. On the other hand, the four aspects mentioned above, have been consistently shown to change regularly with age, independently of such factors as nationality, social class, religion and parental discipline (Kohlberg, 1964). It is interesting that even the permissively reared child at first defines good and bad in terms of punishment.

More recently, Kohlberg (1963a) has re-examined Piaget's notions of moral development in the light of subsequent work in this area. He regards Piaget's central proposition, that there is a regular sequence of developmental stages in the growth of moral judgement, as correct, but finds it necessary to redefine these stages in the light of later evidence. He distinguishes three levels and six stages of moral judgement as follows:

Level I. Pre-moral level:
1. Punishment and obedience orientation (obey rules to avoid punishment).
2. Naïve instrumental hedonism (conform to obtain rewards, have favours returned).

Level II. Morality of conventional rule-conformity:
3. Good-boy morality of maintaining good relations, approval of others (conform to avoid disapproval and dislike by others).
4. Authority-maintaining morality (conform to avoid censure by legitimate authority and the resulting guilt).

Level III. Morality of self-accepted moral principles:
5. Morality of contract and democratically accepted law (conform to maintain the respect of the impartial spectator judging in terms of community welfare).
6. Morality of individual principles of conscience (conform to avoid self-condemnation).

Kohlberg presents evidence that these steps do constitute developmental stages because they show a regular age progression, generality across situations and limited scatter across stages for a particular individual.

While both Piaget and Kohlberg stress the close relationship between the general course of intellectual-cognitive development and the development of moral judgement, neither of them regards the latter as simply a matter of intellectual maturation unaffected by socialization experiences. Piaget regards the essential change in the child's moral judgement as involving a shift from an authoritarian to a democratic ethic associated with a change from social relationships of unilateral respect to relationships of mutual respect. In this connection he emphasizes the fact that the young child is almost completely caught up in his unequal relationship with adults who have all the power and are the source of all rules. His early authoritarian morality is a response to these realities. However, as the child gets older he takes part more and more in peer group relationships which are more nearly like relationships between equals and there he learns the morality of fairness, reciprocity and equality.

Subsequent research has, on the whole, not provided much support for the specific content of Piaget's theory. The aspects of moral judgement which are essential for the distinction between the authoritarian ethic of early childhood and the democratic ethic of later childhood are not the ones for which there is clear evidence of age progression independently of various social background factors. Nevertheless, Piaget's approach implies at least two general propositions which have proved fruitful for recent research. The first of these propositions suggests an intimate link between social and intellectual development, the second specifies the nature of the social factor in moral development as lying in the role-taking opportunities available to the child.

For Piaget, the essence of intellectual development is expressed in the principle of 'decentration', that is, the progressive replacement of a single, limited view of problems by the adoption of many points of view simultaneously. The ability to take other points of view, therefore, lies at the root of intellectual growth. But the ability to take other points of view is closely related to the ability to take the view of others. Imagining how a problem would look from another standpoint is very much like looking at the problem from the perspective of another observer with a standpoint different from one's own momentary one. Thus, intellectual development implies the development of the ability to take the role of the other. But this same ability seems to underlie moral development or, at least, the development of moral judgement. Primitive levels of moral judgement imply a limited capacity of putting oneself in the place of the other person and looking at the situation from his point of view, and each advance in moral development is evidence of a developing capacity to take the role of the other in social relationships. Naturally, there will be certain differences between taking the role of the other in a purely intellectual sense and in a social relationship. But there is an element of overlap in these two functions and it is this which can be assumed to underlie the observed positive correlation between intellectual level and the level of moral judgement in children.

Whatever the part that constitutional factors may play in the development of role-taking abilities, it may be assumed that the child's *opportunities* for role taking constitute a crucial factor in this process. Piaget adopted an oversimplified view of these opportunities, accepting the child's role *vis-à-vis* the parents as inevitably based on unilateral respect, and his role *vis-à-vis* his peers as inevitably based on equality. However, there is really no reason why both types of roles could not be structured in many different ways. Not all parents insist on unilateral respect and not all the child's friends treat him as an equal. It is not the purely external criterion of age difference which determines the nature of the role taken by the child but the actual structure of the relationship, that is, whether the structure is autocratic or democratic. That is why the children of parents who use 'inductive' methods of discipline show a higher degree of moral development (Hoffman and Saltzstein, 1967). Reasoning with the child and explaining the consequences of his actions and intentions creates a different kind of parent–child role system than habitual recourse to punishment. The fact that the parent does not exact retaliation for the consequences of the child's actions but merely requires the child to adopt a certain point of view towards them clearly implies a certain respect for the child's ability to take responsibility for his actions. This respect is lacking in the punitive reaction. In other words, the distinction between induction and sensitization implies a distinction between different levels of mutuality in the parent–child relationship. If ratings of moral maturity have been found to be correlated with such features of family life as confidence sharing, awarding responsibility to the child and sharing in family decisions (Peck and Havighurst, 1960), this is presumably due to the role-taking opportunities which these factors imply for the child. Thus, the importance of parental explanations and methods of discipline lies not in their specific content but in the structuring of the child's role.

Piaget's more fundamental theoretical notions enable one to see yet another analogy between intellectual and moral development. For Piaget, the development of intelligence also implies the development of the *reversibility* of thought, that is, the ability to reverse actions and the effects of actions mentally, so that it becomes possible to think hypothetically. In the field of social relationships, the principle of reciprocity functions in much the same way and in the final analysis all moral judgements come down to different ways of conceiving of the element of reciprocity in human relationships. At the lowest level, reciprocity involves freedom from punishment in return for obedience; and this is followed by the level of exchange of concrete rewards. At a higher level, the reciprocity between specific actions or controls and specific rewards and punishments is replaced by generalized conformity in return for generalized social approval. Finally, the principle of reciprocity is universalized and achieves an autonomous demand value, irrespective of the existence of social sanctions. These levels in the development of conceptions of reciprocity correspond to the levels of moral judgement distinguished by Kohlberg, who also reports a clear relationship between the level of moral judgement of mothers and their children (Kohlberg, 1969).

It is not quite clear, however, whether this 'match' in the level of moral judgement of parent and child is due to explicit teaching or whether it is mediated by the structure which the parent's morality imposes on the child's role. It seems likely that where a parent pays lip service to high moral principles but negates these principles in his relationship to the child, all that the child will learn is the hypocritical use of moral arguments. In general, the problem of hypocrisy is a serious one for cognitive theories of moral development. The ability to engage in high-level moral sophistry is not necessarily a good index of a high level of moral development. The relationship between moral judgement and moral action must also be considered, and it probably depends on somewhat different social antecedents than the development of moral judgement itself.

While the ability to produce abstract moral rationalizations probably depends in large measure on the verbal example of socialization agents, the expression of different kinds of reciprocity in action is much more likely to depend on the previous significant role experiences of the child. In particular, the child's appreciation of the function of reciprocity in human relationships will be shaped by its experience of the reciprocity involved in the mutual demands which he and his parents make on each other. A parent who presses his own demands very strongly but pays little respect to the demands of the child, structures the child's role relationship in such a manner as to leave little scope for the experience of higher levels of reciprocity. The same can be said about the overpermisssive parent who treats the child's demands as paramount. The child's practical experience of reciprocity thus depends on the reciprocity which the parent implicitly recognizes between his own demands and those of his child. This interpretation is in line with research findings which indicate that neither overindulgent nor overpunitive parents are apt to have the most responsible children (Bronfenbrenner, 1961b).

The relationship which the child has with his parents is,

8 Social Attachment and Separation

Attachment

The relationship between a mother and her dependent infant has been viewed as the first and simplest link in the long chain of socialization events. On closer investigation this link is neither as simple nor as immediate as it has been presumed to be.

Although it is not based on direct evidence, there is an influential tradition in psychology which traces the source of the bond between the infant and his mother to some form of 'cupboard love'. It was assumed that the infant's tie to his mother originated in his dependency on her for the gratification of basic needs and primarily the basic need for food. Learning theorists postulated that the mother's appearance became the signal for the gratification of the infant's primary hunger need. Social attachments are, therefore, based on so-called acquired or secondary drives.

More recently the infant has been recognized as making an active contribution in shaping his social environment. The relationship established between a mother and her infant is seen in terms that place greater stress on constitutional and structural factors in the infant.

A renewed interest in what happens inside the organism, and how innate structures or response capacities may be transformed in interaction with the environment, developed largely through the impact of ethological studies and animal experiments. Beginning with the observations of Konrad Lorenz in 1935, 'imprinting' becomes important for hypotheses about the nature and function of attachment behaviour. Imprinting represents a kind of learning that is limited to a fixed period in the infant's development and the results of which are permanent. Lorenz found that there was a specific time in the young gosling's life when exposure to a moving object resulted in the response of following this object. Subsequent investigations have confirmed that these attachments remain remarkably stable through the remainder of the animal's existence. The notion of critical periods of development, which has mainly derived from the findings on imprinting, is based on the assumption that certain skills or responses may never be acquired, or only acquired in impaired form, if optimal environmental conditions are not met within a limited and specific time of an organism's growth. The kind of learning involved in imprinting represents the acquisition of specific stimulus sensitivity for a genetically determined social response.

The term 'primary socialization' is sometimes used instead of 'imprinting' for describing the same kind of learning in mammals (Scott, 1968). Critical periods for becoming attached to a class of moving stimuli have been demonstrated in several species, although the specific time periods differ. The faster animals mature and develop, the earlier the peak period of primary socialization. Substantial evidence that the young of different species will become attached to and follow objects that have never been associated with feeding, comes from many sources. A young lamb, for example, was isolated for six weeks and exposed to a constantly operating television set. After nine weeks of isolation the set was abruptly removed. Immediately the young lamb displayed searching behaviour and promptly approached the set when it was finally found. In other experiments lambs were reared in contact with a dog, but prevented from interacting with it by a wire fence. Here the dog became the attachment figure. The lambs bleated on separation and followed the dog everywhere. Sheep appear particularly prone to form strong and exclusive attachments: orphaned lambs follow humans everywhere and remain unresponsive to sheep, even when returned to the flock at a later stage.

Evidence from animal studies suggests that the end of the period of primary socialization is marked by increasing fear responses to strangers. In human infants the beginning of the period of primary socialization is assumed to commence with the onset of the smiling response. Before the end of the critical period of primary socialization the puppy wags its tail at strangers. The human infant smiles at them. By six months there is a decrease of the smiling rate of babies to strangers, suggesting that the period of primary socialization is nearing an end. It has been found that home-reared babies, in contrast to those reared in orphanages, smile about one week earlier and discriminate against strangers sooner. Studies of children in hospital also support the hypothesis that primary socialization ends at about six or seven months. Older infants engaged in excessive crying when left alone, displayed an increased fear of strangers and clung to the mother continuously when she came to visit them. Once the period of primary socialization is over, a sharply defined attachment to one person, usually the mother, with a decrease in indiscriminate friendliness may be observed (Ainsworth, 1969).

Schaffer and Emerson (1964) who followed the progress of a group of sixty Scottish infants from a few weeks to eighteen months, identified an early phase of 'indiscriminate attachment'. The infants' reactions to a set of separation situations, such as being put down after being held or left alone in the room with a stranger, were observed. In the phase of 'indiscriminate attachment', infants cried when put down after having been held, but the protest was unrelated to the identity of the person from whom they were being separated. At the age of about seven months specific attachments emerged, which became more intense in the following three or four months. However, pronounced individual differences in the onset of specific attachments existed. One infant displayed this kind of behaviour as early as twenty-two weeks, while two of the infants did not exhibit such specific attachment behaviour until after their first birthday. Following the onset of specific attachment there was a rapid increase in the number of persons the babies became attached to. The formation of additional attachment progressed so rapidly that in some infants the forming of multiple attachments seemed to appear simultaneously with the observed specific attachment response.

During the course of this study it was possible to identify some of the variables which were related to the intensity of infants' attachments. The degree of maternal responsiveness, as shown by the mother's readiness to attend to her infant's cry by picking him up and attending to him immediately, was one of the factors involved. The amount of interaction, such as giving the infant a great deal of time and attention besides routine caretaking activities, also played a major role. In general it was observed that any people who provided a great deal of stimulation to the child – even if such people were not involved in fulfilling physiological needs – became attachment figures. The number of figures to whom the child formed attachments was found to be a function of the number of people who interacted with him.

Experimental and observational studies of infants which attempt to identify those conditions under which attachments are formed as well as the differential choices of attachment suggest that some specific kinds of interactions crucially affect development in the first year of life. Tactile stimuli provided by skin contact with the mother, especially those secured through sucking, are of early significance. In the earliest developmental period it has been observed that general distress reactions are allayed by close physical contact, rocking and the opportunity to suck. By the beginning of the second year the visible presence of the mother is sufficient to reduce distress (Cox and Campbell, 1968).

Findings from such studies suggest that clear distinctions must be made between the possible existence of a generalized trait of dependent behaviour and observable specific attachments to particular persons in the young child's life. Attachment behaviour does not necessarily generalize to all other adults. The concept of attachment does not refer to a given class of responses, but to a specific relationship between the child and one particular person. When inferences about the general trait of 'dependence' are made, they are usually based upon observations of behaviour in relation to a special person, such as the mother. Walters and Parke (1965) suggest that it would be wise to substitute the term 'attachment' for the concept of dependency in future discussions of social development. This would shift the focus away from the concept of dependency as a generalized trait toward developmental continuities in social interactions which derive from the attachment system.

Specific attachments are formed in the course of interactions between any two individuals – such as infant and caretaker – in which there is a reciprocal matching of responses involving mutual contact, mutual visual regard or mutual vocalization. Attachment develops most effectively within a transactional framework in which the reciprocal nature of the responses of mother and infant play a major role. Differences have been reported in the extent to which mothers engage in nurturant activities which are geared to the natural rhythms of the infant. Where the mother matched her responses more closely to the current needs of her infant, the establishment of a stronger attachment on the part of the child was observed (Ainsworth and Salter, 1963). Maternal care is complementary to the infant's attachment behaviour. Even in the case of dogs, reciprocal stimulation from puppies is necessary to maintain the appropriate maternal behaviour cycle. Experiments with female rhesus monkeys show that the mother's own early experiences drastically affect her ability to respond to her infant in a reciprocal caretaking manner. Those mothers who had been reared in isolation and were therefore deprived of the mothering experience as infants, neglected and rejected their infants in spite of normal hormonal and physiological changes after giving birth (Harlow and Harlow, 1965).

Bowlby (1969) offers a partial explanation of some of the mechanisms of maternal caring behaviour in the form of a reciprocal feedback system: the infant's innately organized attachment behaviour elicits complementary 'retrieving' behaviour from the mother. The baby is born with six response patterns which increase proximity between a mother and her infant. Crying and smiling initially, and calling at a later stage, bring the mother to her infant. Clinging and sucking at first, with following later on, attach the infant closely to his mother. The early global responses become increasingly differentiated to include a widening range of responses to attract the mother, eliciting retrieving behaviour on her part. The infant probably exerts as much control over his mother's reaction to him as she exerts over his reaction to her (Rosenblatt, 1965).

Such general considerations should not make us forget the peculiarities of each mother–infant pair. As a result of her own personal history, her immediate circumstances and cultural experience, each mother responds to her child in a highly individual manner. Infants also display a wide range of individual differences in the way in which they respond to the environment. This means that there are almost no specific techniques of infant training that can be identified as being intrinsically 'good' or 'bad'. In fact, mother–infant pairs show a surprising degree of variability in establishing satisfactory levels of demands and supports.

Separation

Infants faced with separation from the one person to whom they have become clearly attached have often been observed to decline in a way reminiscent of adults in mourning. The results of these studies have been remarkably uniform. A sequence of typical responses has been noted following the infant's separation from the mother, beginning with much crying and active protest. This is followed by a progressive decline into passive withdrawal from the surroundings and from relationships with other people. The infant is presumed to have 'settled down'. The earlier investigations of the effects of maternal separation describe a progressive depressive syndrome with continuing physical deterioration, in some cases to the point of death.

Not all children, however, reacted to separation with such dramatic signs of disturbance. The quality of the previous relationship of the infant to his mother is one of the key factors determining whether an infant will show more or less severe signs of disturbance. Those infants who have been closely attached to their mother, show the most severe reactions on separation. Secondly, infants who are provided with good substitute maternal care are less drastically affected. Differences in the constitutional sensitivity of infants to stress are also important, though there is always an interaction of these with environmental influences.

An example of the interplay of congenital and environmental factors is provided by the change in the involvement of different sense modalities which may occur when there is a switch from one primary caretaking figure to another. Such changes may result in changes of reward patterns: one nurse may reward the infant with caresses and tactile stimulation while the next may sing and coo to him. Some infants may have a congenitally greater tolerance to change and display a greater flexibility in making new adjustments.

Maternal employment has been considered as a form of partial maternal separation. Various undesirable consequences, including juvenile delinquency, have occasionally been blamed on maternal employment, but closer investigation fails to confirm such harmful effects (Siegel and Haas, 1963). It is common to find no differences in child-rearing attitudes or satisfaction with the homemaker role between working and non-working mothers. However, there is an association between positive attitudes to the maternal role and the role of housewife for both working and non-working mothers. There are many working mothers with positive attitudes to these roles and many non-working mothers with quite negative attitudes. It seems likely that the effect of maternal employment will vary with such maternal attitudes in so far as they affect the quality of the mother's interaction with the child. Maternal attitudes to child rearing are essentially independent of the mother's employment. Where such employment conflicts with feelings of responsibility towards the child, compensatory measures are generally taken. Some working mothers attempt to meet the demands of the infant by a deliberate effort to make up for the possible quantitative deficit caused by absence due to employment.

Accompanying attitudes and institutional settings also determine the effects of multiple mothering, where several people share the caretaking duties in looking after the infant. Here, as in the case of maternal separation, possible negative effects may be caused by extraneous stressful circumstances, as in the case where an unwanted child is shunted from one foster parent to another. In different cultural contexts as, for example, the case of kibbutz children, such adverse effects have not been noted. The meaning of the foster-parent role and the willingness of such substitute caretaking figures to provide the kinds of support normally provided by the mother are decisive in determining the effects of such arrangements on the child.

The effects of maternal separation must be evaluated within the total configuration in which such disturbances take place (Yarrow, 1964). Frequently, the circumstances surrounding separation may be presumed to affect behaviour drastically. In many instances the death of a mother will be followed by removal to an impersonal institution, where the infant is subject to sudden and extreme changes in routine. Separation frequently occurs in the context of other calamities such as economic distress, the disability or illness of a parent, war or natural disasters. The experiences immediately following separation must always be taken into account when interpreting the loss of the mother or other close figure as a causal event in the infant's observed deterioration. Temporary separation from the mother when the infant enters a hospital, is often followed by surgery, unpleasant medication and the discomfort of illness. The way in which a child will respond will depend on his previous experiences, his unique susceptibilities and his ability to interpret events in terms of cause and effect relationships. Separation experiences can only be viewed in relation to concomitant stress. Most children are subjected to separation experiences of greater or lesser degree: the interpretation of such experiences only makes sense within the total configuration.

There has been much speculation about the possible long-term effects of interference with the establishment of early social attachments. Such effects are presumed to express themselves particularly strongly in the quality of later social relationships. The seeds of the so-called sociopathic personality, which is marked by a lack of concern for others, are thought by some to spring from an early disturbance in the mother–child relationship. Retrospective and long-term studies on which such speculations are based have come up with equivocal evidence. There are real difficulties in defining both the nature of the personality disturbances whose antecedents are sought in maternal deprivation and the exact nature of this deprivation itself.

It must also be remembered that the group from which deprived infants come is not a random sample of the general population but generally shows higher incidences of mental deficiency, psychological disturbance and poor economic circumstances. There are some who hold the opinion that genetic factors may be partially responsible for the disturbances which have been observed at a later stage.

The balance of the evidence makes it seem likely that the *cumulative* effects of maternal separation experiences may be manifested in later disturbance, but unlikely that the single separation event leads to particularly marked long-term effects. One cumulative effect of even quite brief periods of separation is an increase in the attachment behaviour of young children (Ainsworth, Salter and Wittig, 1967).

Cases of disturbed individuals with severe separation experiences have become the subjects of dramatically detailed case histories. Less attention has been devoted to the many cases of normally adjusted persons who have overcome traumatic separation reactions. One recorded case in the latter type concerns an illegitimate child who reacted with great distress when she was placed in the Hampstead Nurseries at the age of two (Hellman, 1962). She was described as the child who took the longest to recover from the shock of separation from her mother. Observers who had seen her during the period of severe distress reaction felt that such an event could not pass without leaving a permanent scar on her personality. Nevertheless, the girl made a good subsequent adjustment with no impairment in her ability to form close, long-term relationships. It is interesting that her mother had been brought up in an institution as well. One of the mother's marked personality features was an excellent capacity to make and maintain relationships over a long time. The girl and her mother remained attached to each other through a long period of partial separation.

In assessing the long-term effects of infantile and childhood separation from the mother, the important questions are related to the quality of the pre-separation relationship, the cumulative nature of the separation experience, the quality of substitute relationships, and constitutional factors in the child.

9 Extra-Familial Influences

It is an ironical fact that preoccupation with family influences appears to be most intense in societies where the importance of such influences is in sharp decline. The process of modernization and large-scale industrialization always leads to the growth of new agents of socialization, such as the bureaucratic school and the mass media, which take over many of the functions previously the exclusive concern of kinship units. Inevitably, this historical process is accompanied by a diminution at least in the relative importance of family influences in the total process of socialization. This generates anxiety in parents who find that they have rivals for the child's attention which their own parents and grandparents hardly had to contend with. Perhaps the overwhelming emphasis on parent–child relationships which is so characteristic of research on socialization has its root in this type of concern. At any rate, it must be confessed that the quality and volume of research on extra-familial agents of socialization is only slowly beginning to do justice to the presumed importance of these agents in industrial societies.

Peer groups

Among extra-familial influences, peer groups occupy a somewhat obscure position. While their importance is not so clearly linked to technological development as is the case for the school and the mass media, there are strong suggestions of their increasing importance in industrial societies. Different groups of investigators have attributed observed differences in the behaviour of American youths, on the one hand, and Chinese or Mexican youths, on the other, to the fact that the tyranny of their peers is an experience known only to the former (Hsu, Watrous and Lord, 1960–61; Maslow and Diaz-Guerrero, 1960). However, strong youth groups are certainly not peculiar to technologically developed societies, nor does their importance stand in any simple relationship to the level of industrialization. As Eisenstadt (1956) has observed, youth groups will become important in any society in which family or kinship units are inadequate for ensuring the individual's attainment of full social status. Where the division of labour is not associated with kinship structures, kinship units are ineffective in preparing the individual for important aspects of adult life. Others have pointed out that where educational opportunities are widely available, the family becomes essentially irrelevant to the individual's life chances after the first few years of school. Accordingly, it is not surprising to find that in such communities the amount of time spent in family settings decreases steadily with age, while the time spent in peer-group settings increases (Wright, 1956). Presumably, the effectiveness of the peer group in influencing the behaviour of its members increases concomitantly.

The nature of this influence is, however, exceedingly puzzling. For one thing, its strength will depend on the psychological burden which the child brings into the peer-group setting. A child who is at odds with his parents is more likely to adopt a peer group as a primary source of reference. On the other hand, one of the best documented findings in this area of research refers to the fact that the peer-group setting frequently becomes the avenue for the expression of hostility generated by punitive and restrictive fathers, at least for boys (Bandura and Walters, 1960). Actually, the causal influence of the peer group is extremely difficult to demonstrate unambiguously. Even the well-established relationship between acceptance by peers (popularity) and self-acceptance is merely correlational and allows us to make no causal inferences (Campbell, 1964). It is quite possible that self-confidence leads to popularity, rather than the other way around.

The values and attitudes reinforced by the peer group have often been regarded as running counter to the values of parents and educational authorities. 'Adolescent culture' is said to be anti-intellectual and oriented to consumption rather than work values. Adults in positions of authority often treat the youth culture as an enemy, as a threat to the values which they are trying to transmit. But one suspects that such attitudes usually overlook rather broad areas of agreement between the youth culture and the adult culture, and fasten onto rather superficial differences. If American youth culture is indeed anti-intellectual (Coleman, 1961), this may not be unrelated to the powerful anti-intellectual forces in American adult life which have so frequently been the subject of informed comment. And if a culture strongly values conformity in personal appearance, it is hardly a threat to this value when it expresses itself in an insistence on long hair instead of an insistence on short hair! On the whole, the values of peer-group cultures are much more likely to reinforce the values of the adult world than to oppose them (Elkin and Westley, 1955), however much the rationalizations and superficial expressions of these values may differ. Nevertheless, there are times when a real 'generation conflict' appears; but apart from the obvious case of immigrants who have been transplanted to a different culture, this seems to depend on historical circumstances that require special consideration.

Generations

In so far as men must live out their lives in a changing world, parent and child are separated by a historical gap that is sometimes rather wide. The world which the father entered may have been a very different sort of place from the world that the son contemplates at a similar age. At times of very rapid social change, this may lead to a high degree of estrangement between parents and children. The older generation may feel confused about the behaviour of the younger generation and the latter may feel that the example set by their elders is bad and their experience irrelevant or misleading. Under these circumstances, parents cease to be models for their adolescent children who may turn for confirmation and example to those facing the same kind of future, namely, members of their own generation.

The width of the 'generation gap' will depend on the rapidity of recent social change. Periods of deep political dislocation and change have typically produced a strong sense of generational discontinuity, with groups identifying themselves as 'the revolutionary generation', sometimes taking the label of a critical year, like 1848 in some countries of Central Europe or 1945 in Indonesia.

Recent social psychological studies of sections of American youth (Keniston, 1968) have demonstrated the replacement of elders as models by the consciousness of generation. The focus of identification here is not really a peer group or a political organization, but the generation as such. These youngsters are conspicuously distrustful of formal organizations, indifferent to ideology and their actual peer-group involvements are often unstable. What remains is a strong sense of generational loyalty and a commitment to values which are genuinely personified only in members of one's own generation. There is a pervasive feeling of disconnection from previous generations and their values. This kind of *discontinuity* must be clearly distinguished from youthful *rebellion* which questions the personal position of elders rather than their world. In this case it is a question of wanting to take the elder's place in what is essentially the same world, but genuine generational discontinuity involves a rejection of the value of the place occupied by the elder and a questioning of the structure from which this place gets its meaning.

Kenneth Keniston (1960) has suggested that in the most advanced industrial societies technological change is now proceeding at such a rapid rate that the attendant social changes lead to a state of chronic flux where the future becomes impossible to anticipate and experience of the past becomes obsolete and irrelevant within a very few years.

This may mean 'the end of identification' for those who wish to survive in such a world; there is no point in taking as a model people whose values and ideas have obviously been by-passed by history. More than that, if one expects this state of rapid social change to be permanent, there is an obvious danger in *any* identificatory attachments, except those of a very partial kind. 'With no exemplars, no objects of identification and an obdurate refusal to accept them, the result is often that perplexity, self-fragmentation and confusion we see in many alienated young men' (Keniston, 1960, p. 233).

What is being questioned here is not the existence of early childhood identification with parental models but its continuity with later patterns of identification and its relevance for adult life. Clearly, it will matter to the individual how much opportunity the world provides for acting out an internalized parental image. It also makes a difference whether the parental model is slowly and smoothly replaced by one not altogether dissimilar to it or whether that is made impossible by the inescapable recognition of the absurdity and irrelevance of all such models.

While this point is well taken, the position of youth in contemporary 'post-industrial' society is not as unusual as is sometimes assumed. The state of fragmented identification, alienation and generation gap is characteristic of periods of social dislocation, though the causes of this dislocation may vary from case to case. It may be doubted whether technological change is really relevant here, for many societies have experienced enormous dislocation without any marked technological change; on the other hand, periods of rapid technological advance have sometimes been accompanied by marked social stability. Europe between 1760 and 1910, and Asia in the present century, offer many examples of both types. Certainly, vast generation gaps are no new phenomenon, nor are instances of generational identification unknown before present times. It is also clear that for large numbers of individuals in modern society it is premature to speak of 'the end of identification'.

In the present context, the phrase 'generation gap' merely serves to remind us that the transition from the parental models of identification in early childhood to the adult models of late adolescence is often problematical and may hinge on historical factors that take us far beyond the legitimate concerns of psychology.

Mass media

In the course of the present century, the fairy tale, the film, the comic book and television have in turn been the subject of intensive concern about their possible effects on the young. In each case, it is almost possible to discern a kind of dialectical progress from an early phase of alarm at the evil potentialities of the new medium, through a phase of relief when early research results failed to confirm the worst fears, to a phase of more measured concern about the real effects and limitations of the medium. It may be as well to remind ourselves that an earlier generation of reformers was responsible for the anaemic content of many children's libraries on the grounds that classics like the Grimms' and Andersen's fairy tales were undesirable fare for the young, because of their themes of violence and mistreatment of children. Had they been research-minded, they could undoubtedly have produced evidence that intimidated youngsters were avid consumers of Grimm and Andersen; but who would now put the blame for the youngsters' intimidation on those unfortunate authors? Those who have tried to investigate the effects of films, comic books and television have also found that it is a long step from asserting an association to demonstrating a causal relationship.

It is true that excessive television watching in individual children is a reliable indicator of an escape from real-life problems with which the child cannot cope. In fact, addiction to any of the pictorial media is considered a 'reliable danger signal' and a sufficient reason to explore the possibility of therapeutic action (Maccoby, 1964). But one would hardly wish to take the symptom for the cause. Moreover, such instances tell us nothing about children whose media consumption falls within limits that are considered normal in their community.

There are two ways in which the possible causal effects of the media can be assessed. In the one case, laboratory studies are conducted in which the effect of filmed or other material on children is measured; in the other case, a 'natural experiment' is carried out in a community, where comparable measures can be taken before and after the introduction of a medium like television. Two notable examples of the latter approach are the Norwich study in Britain (Himmelweit, Oppenheim and Vince, 1958) and a similar Japanese study carried out a little later. A comparison of the two shows that the effects of the introduction of television will vary with the general social and cultural context. For example, in Japan, but not in Britain, T V appeared to reduce the reading of serious books and reading ability. Clearly, one must be very careful about generalizing from studies conducted in a particular cultural context. However, it is of interest that both studies agree on the observation that most T V time is taken from time that the children would otherwise have spent with other media or in bed.

Recent experimental studies of the effects of filmed material have concentrated very heavily on violent and aggressive content. In fact, this is perhaps the only aspect of the media-influence problem for which there now exists a respectable body of fairly rigorous research. Many studies of the type described in chapter 3 have shown that young children do imitate the aggressive actions of filmed models as much as live models, that this effect persists over a considerable period of time and is particularly pronounced when the aggressive model is depicted as successful (Bandura, 1965b). Another series of experiments demonstrates that repeated exposure to anxiety-provoking film content blunts emotional response to such content (Lazarus, 1966).

Such findings are quite relevant to real-life TV content in that detailed thematic analysis of popular American programmes has shown (a) that violent methods are the single most popular means employed by characters to reach desired goals and (b) that socially disapproved methods are more frequently portrayed as being successful than are approved methods (Larsen, Gray and Fortas, 1968). 'When the hero guns down the villain, do children really learn that "crime does not pay" or do they learn that it is *good* to kill "bad people"?' (Goranson, 1969, p. 410).

It is unfortunate that research on the cognitive effects of the television medium has been rather neglected. One study did find that the thinking of children with high levels of media exposure was more stereotyped (Bailyn, 1959), but it is not possible to read a causal interpretation into this relationship. Many other possible cognitive effects of television could be suggested. What, for example, is the influence of advertising on language? Does habituation to the phoney appeals of TV commercials undermine confidence in the use of persuasive language in other contexts? What effect, if any, does the extraordinary vividness, credibility and fidelity of the TV medium have on the development of the distinction between fantasy and reality? Is it true that the attitude of passive following required by the medium slows down the development of the child's powers of selective attending? Does the preponderance of vivid, pictorial input delay the development of non-pictorial, logical thinking? These are fascinating questions, but in the present state of our knowledge we can do no more than pose them.

Last, but not least, there is the question of the role which the media play in providing conceptual categories which parents and children use to classify their own experience of themselves and of each other. Adult–child relationships are quite frequently depicted by the mass media, usually in fictionalized form. To what degree are media consumers sensitized by the dominant themes of these representations, so that they experience their own lives in similar terms? In the psychological clinic it sometimes happens that a mother, unfamiliar with psychological jargon, will use the experiences of a favourite T V character to categorize and illustrate her own attitudes or those of her child. To what extent then, do the fictional characters of the T V world serve as models for the definition of social types in the real world of the viewer? This is an important question, for, as Madame Chombart de Lauwe has shown (1970), the process of socialization is shaped by the society as a whole through the power and ubiquity of the culturally sanctioned models presented to the individual. In our age, model parents and children may face a certain amount of competition from their counterparts on television.

Formal education

The role of the school as a socialization agent has been quite extensively studied by educational sociologists and psychologists. In the present context we will restrict ourselves to noting some of the peculiar characteristics that distinguish it from other agents of socialization.

In the first place, it is necessary to distinguish between the socializing functions of the school and other important functions, like social *selection*. It would be a mistake to regard the school as being primarily a socializing agent. With the decline of hereditary privilege, that function has become distinctly secondary to the function of assigning social positions to individuals, of determining what range of occupations shall be available to an individual. In other words, it is primarily an agent of social mobility and its socialization functions are often subordinated to this fundamental concern. Among other things, the school system presents the child with a simulated model of the bureaucratic society in which he will have to take his place as an adult and it does this not only as a form of training or preparation, but in order to gauge the child's ability to adopt to the demands of such a social system. The first distinction between school and family, therefore, is that in the former the child is essentially *on test* – his status depends on measurable achievement. This is different in the family, where his status is much more determined by 'ascribed' characteristics like age, sex, personal qualities, etc.

In the school, the child is for the first time exposed to controlling adults, whose reactions to him are severely circumscribed by a system of precise written rules, the essence of bureaucracy. While the heavy and widespread reliance of mothers on the written child-training prescriptions of Dr Spock or his equivalents makes their influence approximate the force of administrative rules, there remains at least a difference of degree in the two cases. Personal idiosyncrasy plays a bigger role even for the most book-bound and rule-bound mother, than it does for the average teacher or school principal. For one thing, the amount of time available for interaction between the adult and the individual child is generally much smaller at school than at home, so that the development of individualized relationships is severely hampered. What the school does is to facilitate the transition from personal to positional modelling, described in chapter 3. This is institutionalized in the change from the class teacher of the early years to the subject teacher of the later school years. The more impersonal, task-oriented and businesslike the teacher, the more he is likely to accelerate this development.

It was pointed out in chapter 3 that positional modelling is facilitated by the perceived legitimized power position of the model in a social system and not by the personal threat of the model's power over the child. The teacher who is personally punitive, therefore, undermines his own position as a model. The kind of positional identification which manifests itself as respect for the teacher is likely to be furthered by the teacher's perceived competence at the task assigned to him by the system. Perhaps this is part of the reason for the demonstrated greater effectiveness of teachers with a more abstract level of cognitive functioning

(Harvey *et al.*, 1966). However, the perception of this kind of competence assumes an acceptance of the legitimacy and validity of the values of the educational system on the part of the child. This is something that has been repeatedly shown to be linked to social class. On the whole, middle-class parents are more likely to share and support the values of the school system than are working-class parents, and it is those working-class children whose families atypically support the values of formal education that are likely to do well at school and to become socially upward mobile.

Those children who do not identify with the teacher nor accept the values of the system will seek to validate their position by the concensus of their peers, the more successfully the larger the proportion of those in their immediate environment who share their background. In a working-class area the teacher may, therefore, find himself opposed by a solid wall of apathy and resentment. This development is promoted by the typical juxtaposition of formal and informal relationships, which the school shares with other bureaucratically organized institutions. The formation of informal groups that oppose 'the system' more or less successfully is, of course, an invariable consequence of formal organization, whether in the army, the civil service, the large industrial corporation or the school. But it is at school that the individual is first confronted with this ubiquitous phenomenon in a pure form, a socialization experience of no mean importance. He is forced to make his choice and to define his commitments in respect to the rival claims of formal authority and informal group. His spontaneous youthful decisions, while not necessarily irrevocable, are at least statistically linked to his subsequent life chances. The 'bifurcation' of the school class into rebels and teachers' pets is perhaps the most consequential stimulus to socialization in late childhood.

Like all formal organizations the educational bureaucracy is forever seeking to manipulate the informal cells that it spawns, so as to transform them from potential sources of

10 Social Class

Social-class differences in the abilities, motives and values of children are too well known to require elaborate documentation in the present context. It may be assumed that working-class children will statistically tend to do less well than middle-class children on conventional intelligence tests, will have lower levels of educational and occupational aspiration and will be less in tune with the middle-class orientation of the educational system.

The catalogue of social-class differences has been further extended by evidence garnered in psychological laboratories, although this source of data has generally led to inconsistent and even mutually contradictory findings. Thus, some studies suggest that working-class children are less influenced by symbolic rewards than middle-class children (Zigler and de Labry, 1962), but others report no class differences in the effectiveness of verbal and non-verbal rewards (Spence and Segner, 1967). Supposed class differences in the effectiveness of various kinds of verbal reward have also not been confirmed (Rosenhan and Greenwald, 1965).

Unfortunately, this type of research throws no light on the nature of social-class differences in socialization, because even if a body of consistent findings existed it would be open to many different interpretations. There is evidence that middle-class children react more placidly than working-class children to middle-class psychologists in their middle-class institutional environment (Rosenhan, 1966), hence we do not know whether class differences in this setting have any bearing on class differences outside. Moreover, the mere establishment of class differences tells us nothing about the process of socialization of which they may be a product. In recent years there has, therefore, been less interest in a catalogue of class differences and more concern with the question of how they come about.

It is not difficult to point to obvious environmental differences that are generally linked to social class and that can be expected to affect the development of the child. Crowded living conditions, relatively large family size, lack of access to literary resources, etc., are often characteristic of working-class families and their effects pose no great difficulties of interpretation. More subtle and interesting are the effects of differences in sex roles and in the authority structure of the family, as well as the relative importance of siblings and peers versus parents as agents of socialization. However, these factors are best considered in their own right, leaving the question of their possible correlation with social class as an extraneous, sociological, consideration.

Another source of class differences which has received much emphasis in practical contexts can be identified with the cognitive deprivation that many lower-class children are exposed to (Deutsch and Deutsch, 1968). Their environment frequently lacks those elements of stimulation which are necessary for rapid cognitive development. Cognitively more advanced children tend to come from homes where there are more books and where adults read more books to children and converse with them during meals (Milner, 1951).

Considerable research has been devoted to class differences in the quality of parent–child relationships. The basis for these differences has been sought in several different aspects of the relationship.

Firstly, it is clear that middle- and working-class parents may provide different models for the child to follow. In so far as there are class-linked differences among adults in regard to values as well as cognitive and effective functions, children of different class background will be exposed to the influence of different models. A professional father who expresses somewhat intellectual values in his behaviour will induce different behaviour in his son than a father who actually opposes such values in word and deed. It has been shown experimentally that children will emulate the standards of goal achievement which adult models set themselves. For instance, in a ring toss game they will impose either strict or permissive standards on themselves, depending on the relevant behaviour of the previously observed adult model (Bandura, Grusec and Menlove, 1967). It is possible, therefore, that class-linked differences in parental standards, norms and values for various situations may be transmitted simply by observational learning.

If it is true that the effectiveness of a model in observational learning varies with its social power (see chapter 3), then some difference in the effectiveness of middle- and working-class fathers may be expected. In general, middle-class and working-class fathers do not have the same degree of power outside the family and when the child is old enough to become sensitive to this a change in the effectiveness of the paternal model may occur. Many working-class fathers may have to face more challenges to the legitimacy of their authority than those middle-class fathers who can demonstrate the importance of their social position.

One approach to the study of class differences in socialization is to investigate parental goals. In other words, middle- and working-class parents may be regarded as making differing kinds of demands on their children. Their demands will concern matters that they regard as both important and problematical, in the sense that they cannot take it for granted that the child will develop in the desired direction. Now, what is considered both important and problematical is not the same for middle- and working-class parents. For example, there is fairly good evidence to suggest that while working-class parents are more concerned to impose demands for obedience, middle-class parents are more concerned about the problems and virtues of self-control (Kohn, 1959). M. Kohn has pointed out that this difference runs parallel to the difference between middle-class and working-class occupations. The former generally require more self-direction, while the latter require submitting to direct supervision and following explicit rules laid down by someone in authority. It is assumed that these differences will lead to a different value orientation among parents varying in class background and that these values will prescribe the goals they seek to achieve in training their children. From this point of view, what is important is not the question of whether a given technique of discipline, like physical punishment, is used more often by parents in one class than in another, but rather the different context in which it is used.

Working-class parents are apt to resort to physical punishment when the direct and immediate consequences of their children's disobedient acts are most extreme, and to refrain from punishing when this might provoke an even greater disturbance. Thus, they will punish a child for wild play when the furniture is damaged or the noise level becomes intolerable, but ignore the same actions when the direct and immediate consequences are not so extreme. Middle-class parents, on the other hand, seem to punish or refrain from punishing on the basis of their interpretation of the child's intent in acting as he does. Thus, they will punish a furious outburst when the context is such that they interpret it to be a loss of self-control, but will ignore an equally extreme outburst when the context is such that they interpret it to be merely an emotional release.

It is understandable that working-class parents react to the consequences rather than to the intent of their children's actions: the important thing is that the child does not transgress externally imposed rules. Correspondingly, if middle-class parents are instead concerned about the child's motives and feelings, they can and must look beyond the overt to why the child acts as he does. It would seem that middle- and working-class values direct parents to see their children's misbehaviour in quite different ways, so that misbehaviour which prompts middle-class parents to action does not seem as important to working-class parents, and vice versa (Kohn, 1963, p. 478).

While broad differences in parental values may be important

for understanding some overall class differences in the nature of parental demands, they do not enable us to explain how the orientation of the parent is in fact communicated to the child. Early attempts to come to grips with this issue relied mainly on questioning mothers about the techniques of discipline they thought they employed.

Unfortunately, most of these studies have very serious methodological weaknesses which include excessive reliance on interview techniques known to be unreliable, poor sampling, lack of equivalence between questions asked in different studies, ambiguity in the questions themselves, excessive attention to superficial aspects of behaviour, lack of controls for some key background variables – and much more besides. Under these circumstances it is not surprising that findings in this area present a confused and totally inconsistent picture (Clausen and Williams, 1963) and that research of this kind has hardly been pursued in recent years (Hess, 1970).

A more promising line of approach is presented by an increasing number of studies based on direct and systematic observation of mother–child interaction. There is considerable convergence in the findings from several of these studies. It appears that (at least in the United States) working-class mothers are less inclined to engage in verbal communication with their children (Zunich, 1961) and are less responsive to requests made by the child (Kamii and Radin, 1967). There are also some very interesting differences in the quality of verbal interaction. When mothers were observed teaching their four-year-old children simple tasks, the middle-class mothers were inclined to be more specific in their instructions, to request more verbal feedback, to provide more information and to monitor their children's performance more effectively (Hess and Shipman, 1967).

Such findings clearly point to the importance of the use of language as a medium for structuring the cognitive world of the child. In interacting with their children, parents differing in class background are apt to use language in different ways to influence the behaviour of the child. In the studies just mentioned, working-class mothers were more inclined to call the child's attention to status or normative considerations, requesting compliance on the basis of rules laid down by someone in authority. This is congruent with descriptive studies that indicate an early tendency for working-class individuals to adapt to situations where they are in a subordinate position, being acted upon by persons in authority whose behaviour they are powerless to influence effectively. Among other things, this may lead to a general tendency to place more emphasis on the power component in human relationships (Kohn, 1969) and to develop a sense of low self-esteem, inefficacy and passivity (Rosenberg, 1965).

To return to class differences in the use of language, it appears that the middle-class mother is likely to use a wider range of words, expressing finer discriminations, to use a more complex syntactic structure which makes more demands on the child's cognitive ability and to rely less on non-verbal channels of communication. Bernstein (1964) has attempted to give a systematic description of these differences in terms of his distinction between elaborated and restricted codes. Briefly, the latter are characterized by stereotype of expression, lack of precision, simple and unfinished sentences, frequent shifts of subject and implicit rather than explicit meaning. Elaborated codes involve a more differentiated, more complex and more precise communication of meaning. It is also suggested that these codes express different kinds of social relationships. The use of restricted codes implies an attempt at social control by an appeal to social status, while elaborated codes have to be used if social control is to be exercised by an appeal to reason. It is the difference between the mother who says 'Shut up' and the mother who says, 'Would you mind keeping quiet? I can't hear what this gentleman is saying.'

Bernstein goes on to suggest that these different patterns

of communication may have far-reaching psychological consequences for the child. In the main, verbal mediation will play a bigger role in the life of the child accustomed to elaborated codes. This means that he is better able to verbalize and hence to react to his own intentions and feelings, that he is more affected by symbolically presented distant goals and that he is able to work out a more extended and more complex sequence of rationally linked goals and subgoals. This would account for the well-known class differences in educational and career aspirations.

In practice, the empirical verification of this very elaborate chain of hypotheses presents many problems. However, class differences in the use of language by parents and children have often been demonstrated and many of these differences can be accommodated by the distinction between elaborated and restricted codes. For instance, it has been shown that in explaining tasks to the child (Hess and Shipman, 1965) and in answering the child's questions (Robinson and Rackstraw, 1967), middle-class mothers do exhibit slightly more of the linguistic characteristics of elaborated codes than working-class mothers. One recent study also demonstrated that the tone in which words like 'good', 'right', 'bad' and 'wrong' were spoken was crucial for their effect on the behaviour of young working-class children but not for middle-class children who responded to the verbal meaning irrespective of tonal inflection (Brooks, Brandt and Wiener, 1969). Presumably, these children showed the effect of differential experience in the use of words by their parents.

The precise significance of such class differences in verbal communication between parents and children remains to be firmly established. It is an open question whether linguistic differences can be directly related to patterns of parental power assertion or authority. Until the latter variable is independently assessed or manipulated there is no way of testing the relationship that is claimed to exist. At this stage, the psychological consequences of class-linked differences in language usage also remain essentially a matter for conjecture. The mere co-existence of psychological and linguistic differences among children of differing class backgrounds does not, of course, enable us to draw any causal inferences. A great deal of work on the mediating role of language needs to be done before we are in a position to verify speculations about the psychological significance of social-class differences in verbal communication. It is clear, however, that work in this area offers exciting possibilities of new insights and of practical gains for the process of public education.

11 Cross-Cultural and Historical Studies of Socialization

In any society there is likely to be some relationship between the norms operating in parent–child relationships and other aspects of the life of that society. As one might expect, parents who want to train hunters stress different virtues than parents who want to perpetuate a race of settled peasants. Nor would it come as a surprise to learn that parents with strong culturally determined beliefs in a harsh spirit world treat their own children somewhat harshly. The socialization process hardly exists in a cultural vacuum and its elements will always be affected by elements in the wider culture.

The literature of cultural anthropology and of anthropological journalism is not lacking in accounts of cross-national differences in child training, some of them brash and unreliable, others sensitive and perceptive. Unfortunately, the step from these twentieth-century versions of traveller's tales to systematic research on the role of cultural factors in the parent–child relationship has proved to be a most difficult one to take and two decades of effort have yielded little but an improved understanding of the many pitfalls that await the research worker in this area.

In the first place, one must be in a position to defend one's observations against the criticism that the sample on which they are based is not representative of the population about which one is trying to generalize. This is particularly important for descriptive studies of 'modal' patterns of child training and personality. In fact, this is the rock upon which all the older studies of culture and personality have foundered. Detailed observations of infant-feeding practices in a remote mountain village are hardly a reliable basis for generalizing about a whole nation and studies of the childhood experiences of political refugees are a flimsy foundation for generalizations about the psychological meaning of a particular political system.

The 'modal' personality or child-training pattern, which is somehow characteristic of a given cultural group is in fact a will-o'-the-wisp which will ever elude our grasp. Once we get beyond the tiniest groups the problems of adequate sampling become immense and the more allowance we make for the existence of sub-cultural differences the more chimerical the modal cultural pattern becomes (Berrien, 1967).

Modern research has, therefore, concentrated on the analysis of cross-cultural differences rather than on modal, descriptive studies. For this purpose it is much more important that the samples be comparable than that they are representative. Comparability would involve such parameters as age, occupation, educational level, urban or rural origin, etc. Because culturally heterogeneous populations frequently differ on such parameters, the matching of samples in the interests of comparability usually leads to unrepresentativeness in at least one of the samples. On the other hand, representative samples are frequently not comparable because the populations differ so much on a number of parameters. In that case it becomes impossible to disentangle the influence of cultural differences from a host of other social influences.

If one wants to be ambitious and to make broad generalizations about the significance of institutions found in many cultures, such as incest taboos or initiation rites, one ought to be careful about one's sample of cultures as well as one's sample of persons within each culture. One reason for the shakiness of findings in this area is that the sampling of cultures is usually quite arbitrary and in no way affected by rational considerations.

But even if these aspects of the sampling problem were to

receive the most careful attention, the more intractable problem of ensuring comparability with respect to the social situations sampled would remain. To assess the psychological significance of cultural influences on various aspects of human behaviour it is necessary to be certain of the functional equivalence of the same behaviour in different cultures (Frijda and Jahoda, 1966). Similar activities frequently have a different psychological significance in different societies. For instance, it is difficult to know what to make of the simple finding that average T V viewing time is seven hours per week for East German children, compared to twenty to twenty-five hours for American children (Kurth, 1964), unless we also know a great deal about the function of T V viewing among children in both societies. Even the most common activities used to obtain psychological data, such as conversation (e.g. in an interview) and the production of fantasy, will have somewhat different social functions in different societies; they are not psychologically equivalent across cultures. This means that cross-cultural differences may simply reflect variations in the social functions of an activity rather than psychological differences.

Such considerations make any interpretation of correlations between child-training practices and social institutions extremely risky. Correlations of this kind have been discovered by an examination of diverse descriptive accounts of a large number of human groups, with a pre-industrial and rural character (Whiting, 1954). These correlations are of two kinds. On the one hand, there are correlations between features of the group's economic life and their reported child-training values. For instance, hunters are more likely to stress independence training than are settled peasants who store food after it is harvested (Barry, Child and Bacon, 1959). On the other hand, there are correlations between child-training practices and cultural values expressed in artistic, religious or magical forms. Because of the functional non-equivalence of these forms from one society to another, the existence of such correlations tells us nothing about the relationship between childhood experience and personality. Such inferences would have to be based on a completely unjustified equation of personality and culture. Moreover, the cultural system is itself extremely complex and it is strongly influenced by its social and economic context. Hence, it is always possible to give several interpretations to any given correlation taken out of context (Young, 1962).

In order to use cross-cultural data to obtain new insights into the socialization process it would be necessary to take psychological measurements that retain their validity in spite of cultural differences. In view of the very poor showing of available techniques of personality assessment in a single culture (Vernon, 1964), this further complication is likely to lead into a methodological swamp from which extrication will be laborious and slow. In general, the problems of cross-cultural research become greater the heavier the reliance on language. It is, therefore, to be expected that, for the time being, most of the useful substantive findings in this field will come from studies of infants and of non-verbal functions. Nevertheless, other studies must continue, because we will never improve our methods unless we make plenty of mistakes from which we can learn.

One of the major goals of cross-cultural investigations of socialization practices has been the search for universal and 'pancultural' dimensions of parent–child relationships. If factors like 'maternal warmth' or 'authoritarianism' could be unambiguously identified in many cultures and could be demonstrated to run through many specific forms of parent –child interaction, they would give us a relatively stable framework of basic dimensions for categorizing such interaction. Accordingly a number of investigators have subjected data in this area to factor analysis. As might have been expected, the factors they have emerged with vary from one study to another and do not give the slightest promise of providing a stable conceptual framework. The only possible exceptions appear to be the very general factors of parental warmth or affection and parental control of the child (Peterson and Migliorino, 1967). These factors are, of course, known from other studies which were not cross-cultural and can probably be interpreted as constituting a measure of parental demands on the child and of parental effectiveness in meeting the demands of the child (see chapter 5). While such cross-cultural confirmation of the fundamental coordinates of the parent–child system is not without some value, it does not provide the more detailed framework necessary for a better comprehension of intercultural variation.

Further progress in this area would seem to depend on detailed studies of specific aspects of the parent–child relationship. For example, the existing literature suggests that when compared to parents from other cultures American parents may be 'grossly deviant' (as one writer expresses it) in the extent to which they encourage aggression against peers. This type of finding is of some intrinsic interest and further research into its sources and implications would seem to be well worth while. Such limited research goals would, of course, imply a break with the rather unfortunate tradition that treats the culture of a group as a unitary cause to which the most far-flung effects are traced. In fact, the unity and consistency of cultural orientations has almost certainly been grossly overrated in the past. For example, it becomes difficult to distinguish German and American parents on some global orientation of 'authoritarianism' in the light of the finding that while German parents are more controlling in such areas as toilet training and table manners, American parents are more controlling in such areas as sex behaviour, personal hygiene and sports (Karr and Wesley, 1966).

Perhaps the most valuable function of cross-cultural research on socialization is the widening of the investigator's horizon. As he is not immune to the influences of his own culture he is likely to frame his questions in the terms that he has come to take for granted. He will look for differences among parents and children on the dimensions that define problematic areas for his culture, areas like dependency, for example. When he attempts to extend his investigation to other cultures, he may find that there are no equivalent terms for defining his major variables in other languages and practically no variation of behaviour on his chosen dimensions. On the other hand, if he keeps his eyes and ears open and knows how to work with people whose background differs from his own, he will discover the existence of psychologically significant variations on dimensions of child training which experience in his own culture would not have led him to expect. For example, if he comes from a culture with strong puritan traditions he may fail to anticipate significant variation in regard to parental attitudes to such matters as public nudity and public elimination behaviour among children. He may even become aware of dimensions of parent–child interaction that define problems different from the ones which beset his own culture. For example, the dimension of 'respect' which exists where parent–child relations are given a high degree of formal structure is certainly different from the problem of authoritarianism which arises when this formal structure receives little or no cultural sanction. If cross-cultural research helps us to recognize that many of our most popular questions about parent–child relationships are meaningful only within a limited cultural orientation, it will have paid its way.

Many of the most intractable problems of cross-cultural studies of socialization stem from a static model of culture and of childhood that is completely unrealistic. None of the cultures that have been studied in this context are unaffected by constant internal changes and these changes affect parent–child relationships as much as anything else. The traveller who returns to the same society a generation later is usually surprised by the depth and extent of these changes (Mead, 1956). Therefore, the cross-sectional comparison of societies at a particular point in time has something very accidental about it. It is like the comparison of a number of stills, chosen at random from various films. The unity of theme of each film is most likely to escape us, because it is a unity of sequence that necessarily requires the dimension of time to make it comprehensible. Lacking this element, one is likely to see only meaningless variety or to impose a false unity that lacks movement. In reality, variety is often the by-product of social change, because the different parts of a culture do not change at the same rate. The comparison of data from the same source, but of different historical date, therefore offers a methodology that is much more likely to yield meaningful results than a purely cross-sectional approach.

Documents provide one convenient source of data for studies of this type, especially in highly developed societies with their abundant child-care literature. Thus, one well-known study has examined successive editions of the United States Children's Bureau bulletin *Infant Care* between the years 1914 and 1951 (Wolfenstein, 1953). The analysis concentrated on the relative severity or mildness in handling the child's impulses in the areas of thumb sucking, masturbation, weaning and toilet training. Certain very clear trends appeared. In the first two bulletins (1914 and 1921) mothers are advised to treat thumb sucking and masturbation with great severity – sleeves must be sewed down over 'the offending hand', legs must be tied down, etc. The treatment is entirely mechanical and peripheral. In the 1929 bulletin the child's auto-erotic drives are no longer regarded as quite so dangerous and treatment by diversion is recommended. However, the focus of severity now shifts to toilet training which is to be begun almost at birth and to follow a rigid schedule which is not to vary by as much as five minutes. A rigid schedule is also to govern the weaning process, irrespective of the child's demands.

From 1938 to 1951 a very marked trend in the direction of increasing mildness in the treatment of infants can be detected. Auto-erotic activities become harmless and trivial, the tempo of weaning (at least from 1942 onwards) is to be adapted to individual needs rather than following a preconceived schedule and toilet training becomes a matter of training the mother rather than the child.

The analysis of documentary material relevant to child training need not be limited to the present century. For example, a study of advice on child rearing in the medical literature has been made, going back to the sixteenth century (Ryerson, 1961). There is a strong indication of a dramatic change in this advice with the onset of industrialization. Whereas before the middle of the eighteenth century the recommended treatment of infants was permissive, an overwhelming emphasis on strictness and control develops during the following period and lasts well into the present century. In the early period babies were to be fed on demand, weaning was to take place at about two years of age and was to be gradual, toilet training was not to be undertaken during the first year of life and the child was not expected to be consistently dry at night until the age of five; no prohibitions against nudity or infantile sexuality are mentioned; the child remained in his mother's bed until weaning and was put to sleep by rocking; he was freely handled and petted by adults and his crying met with a quick and nurturant response. By the early nineteenth century the picture is entirely different. The age of weaning is reduced, feeding schedules are introduced, toilet training is to be begun and completed much earlier; infantile sexuality is to be punished (this becomes general only in the last part of the nineteenth century); rocking, cuddling and an indulgent response to the baby's cry are disapproved of; on the other hand, the child's free motor activity was now encouraged, whereas previously it had been discouraged. A necessarily crude comparison of these data with observations collected in seventy-five different societies across the world strongly suggests that the severity of the nineteenth century was rather unusual in terms of the human norm, whereas the earlier advice was much more in line with the general practice of mankind.

Speculation about the reasons for such historical changes would take us far beyond the scope of this book. It is always possible to point to simultaneous ideological changes of a more general kind, such as the spreading influence of Wesleyan Methodism in the eighteenth and early nineteenth century. At the same time, changes in family structure must clearly be related to the kind of treatment the child receives. The change from an extended family household to the nuclear family places greater demands on the mother, increases the value of the individual child for the parents and creates greater intimacy between child and parent. It is possible that factors such as these lead to an emphasis on an earlier training of the child as well as to an increased salience of the incest taboo and everything connected with it.

To what extent can one assume a correspondence between authoritative advice on child rearing and actual parental practices? Direct information on this point is sparse and interviews with parents would not be of much use because of the tendency to give the socially desirable response which will often be the one favoured by the expert authorities. The Fels Research Institute in America has systematic data based on the observation and rating of mother–child interaction over a considerable period of time. The files of the Institute have been examined for broad historical trends in the period 1939 to 1961 and a general reduction in maternal coerciveness for this period has been shown (Walters and Crandall, 1964). This would seem to follow the changes in the child-care literature that have already been mentioned, although the mothers in the sample may have been atypical in the amount of attention they paid to this literature. It has been shown that apparent inconsistencies in the findings of studies of child rearing carried out at different times can be explained by the assumption that middle-class mothers respond to printed advice more quickly and more completely than working-class mothers (Bronfenbrenner, 1958b). While this is probably true, a gradual diffusion of new ideas about child training is likely in a society where there is a certain amount of social mobility.

There is a danger in studies of changes in parental practices over time that limited evidence will be used to draw general conclusions. It is obvious that a similar underlying attitude may manifest itself now in one area of child rearing, now in another. The fashion may be for parental severity to express itself in the handling of infantile sexuality during one period and in the handling of toilet training during another period. Such changes in fads must be distinguished from more general changes that affect practically all aspects of the parent–child relationship.

For an understanding of the significance of these broader and slower changes it will be necessary to go beyond documentary evidence to consider developments in art, in dress, in customs and so on. Changes in the way in which children are painted and included in paintings, changes in their dress and in their games, and changes in generally recognized manners and customs pertaining to parent–child relationships provide a rich source of data for hypotheses that help to expand the horizon of current research. Philippe Aries's (1962) brilliant analysis of the historical evidence leads to the conclusion that the stages of individual development which are recognized by cultural convention depend on the existence of specific social institutions. Thus, childhood itself is not a clearly distinguished concept until the advent of social institutions, notably the modern school and the bourgeois family, which create specific roles for it. Before this, the transition from infancy to participation in the activities of adults was rather abrupt; not only did the medieval school not cater to a specific age group, but the children of those times were indiscriminately drawn into the social and economic activities of their elders. From this perspective the current scientific interest in child development, socialization, and the influence of childhood experience on adult behaviour, can be seen as the most recent stage in a long historical process which involves the progressive articulation of a sphere of private life that is distinct from the kind of life in public that is still characteristic of a large part of mankind.

12 Research Methodology – A Critical View

The unreliability of mothers

If questions are to be asked about the child's socialization, what could be more natural than to ask the mother? She is surely the perfect observer on the spot, able to supply a detailed account of the child's life based on the most intimate and uninterrupted acquaintance. At least, so it seemed to the early students of this field.

Unfortunately, the considerable investment of time and money in interviewing mothers that characterized the socialization research of the forties and fifties has established little beyond the almost total unreliability of maternal reports. When the mother's answers to questions about her child were compared with independent observations and factual records an embarrassing gap invariably appeared. For instance, in one critical re-assessment over two hundred mothers were questioned about their children who had attended a research nursery school several years previously (Yarrow, Campbell and Burton, 1968). At that time detailed case records were kept and these could subsequently be compared with the mother's recollections. Perhaps no one would be surprised to learn that the mothers' reports about the child's earlier social life bore little or no relation to the impressions recorded by independent observers at the time the child was of pre-school age. While the ratings made by several uninvolved observers showed an impressive degree of agreement (correlations were generally above 0·8), the correlation of these ratings with the mother's recollections dropped to negligible levels (coefficients between 0·2 and 0·4). Indeed, it would be naïve to expect 'objective' ratings of the child's social relationships from its mother at the time, let alone several years later.

What is more surprising and disturbing is that the mothers proved to be such poor informants even about relatively objective and factual matters like the child's health (correlation 0·39), his sleeping habits (correlation 0·26) and early childhood traumata (correlation 0·39) (Yarrow, Campbell and Burton, 1964). Of course, the known facts about the frailty of human recollection of personally coloured events should have made one anticipate such findings. The lesson to be learned is that even facts which can be precisely recorded by an outside observer are subject to a high degree of distortion in the memory of someone as intimately involved as a mother in the life of her child. To make matters worse, there are enormous individual differences among mothers in respect to the consistency of their reports from one interview to another (Haggard, Brekstad and Skard, 1960). This is likely to lead to spurious correlations where data from mothers' interviews provide the sole source of research data.

The distortions in maternal reports are not random but follow certain directions dictated by the desire to present a favourable image. The trouble with the research interview is that the purposes of the two people involved are quite divergent. The psychologist is trying to get at what he regards as the objective truth, the mother being interviewed is much more likely to be concerned with making a good impression. Abstract generalizations about parent–child relationships have little intrinsic interest for her when it is a matter of presenting to a stranger an acceptable account of matters that may touch on the very core of her own life. Questions about her child's behaviour and about her relationship to the child are seen to involve implicit judgements of her adequacy. These are matters for which she feels personally responsible, not neutral matters of fact. It is almost impossible to question a normal mother about these things without also implicitly questioning her performance in what is perhaps the central relationship in her life.

The content of the research interview practically guarantees an irrevocably defensive attitude on the part of the mother, and attempts by the interviewer to put her at her ease are likely to have at best a superficial effect. Thus, even highly trained and skilful interviewers very rarely obtain admissions of punitive, rejecting and hostile behaviour on the part of the mother or of the child. In fact, a comparison of the incidence of such reports by mothers with reports by trained observers of family interaction clearly shows that such matters are very effectively suppressed (McCord and McCord, 1961). Moreover, such comparisons reveal a general tendency for the mother's verbal avowals to be much closer to the prevailing cultural stereotype of the 'good mother' than to reality. For the middle-class mother, the stereotype is apt to be a close reflection of whatever happens to be the prevailing fashion in the currently popular child-training literature (Robbins, 1963).

Given some fairly consistent individual differences among mothers in their susceptibility to these effects of 'social desirability', spurious correlations between reported maternal behaviour and reported child behaviour are bound to arise. For instance, if the same mothers who describe themselves as warm and affectionate with their children also describe their children as responsible it does not follow that the one variable is any sense the 'cause' of the other. It is much more likely to be the case that answers to both sets of questions are essentially determined by the degree of the mother's preoccupation with social desirability in the interview situation.

But quite apart from the unreliability of the mother's report, it is necessary to question her ability to make the relevant observations in the first place. In order to give a true account of her own behaviour towards her child she would first have to observe it accurately – a tall order indeed, when we remember how vague people are apt to be about their own behaviour in much less involving situations. Let us suppose the mother is answering a question about her praise of the child. Is it really to be supposed that her answer will be based on a careful internal record of all her little exclamations of 'fine', 'good', etc? Of course not! For one thing, she is probably unaware of these reactions a large part of the time and if she did keep a record of them the oddness of her personality would far outweigh any effect of the praise reactions as such. In the normal case, the mother's verbal report would certainly tell us something about her conscious intentions, but it is doubtful that it would tell us anything about her actual behaviour.

In many ways, the mother's report suffers from the same limitations as the introspective report in general psychology. While it cannot fulfil the role of the major source of data for the discipline, it has its place as an auxiliary technique. For example, it may be instructive to make a systematic study of deviations between mothers' reports and direct observations of parent–child interactions, or of children's responses. But recent years have seen a reluctance on the part of many students of socialization to make even this concession to the mother interview. In fact, the field has experienced something of a belated behaviourist revolt, leading to a spate of laboratory studies that are intended to supply the unambiguous answers that interview methods failed to provide.

Laboratory research

The shift to laboratory research in the area of socialization involves three major changes of approach. In the first place, the roles of 'observer' and of 'subject of observation' are rigidly separated and never played by the same person. Where mothers' reports of their own behaviour are taken as primary data, this is clearly not the case, for here the mother is both the observer of her own behaviour and the subject of that observation. To escape the undesirable consequences of this confusion, which were outlined in the

previous section, it has seemed necessary to award the
mother solely the role of subject, reserving the role of
observer for the research worker. By analogy we may remind ourselves of the early days of experimental psychology when one and the same person, for example Ebbing-
haus, served as both the experimenter and the subject of the
experiment. Later, these roles were almost invariably separated. In socialization research this has meant the replacement of mother interviews by direct observations of mother–
child interaction.

In many cases, a second innovation has been introduced,
namely, the control of certain aspects of the setting in
which the interaction takes place. Instead of simply observ-
ing mother and child in the setting of their own home, they
have been called to the laboratory, where they can be presented with carefully prepared tasks and where extensive
recordings can be made. For example, mother and child
may be separately presented with a problem to which various
solutions are possible (Greenglass, 1971). They may be
asked to interpret a picture or to choose one among a set of
objects to take home. Frequently, their solutions and choices
will diverge – the child may choose a record and the mother
a tea towel, for instance. Then they are confronted with the
divergence and asked to reach agreement among themselves
– they may take home one or other object, but not both.
Their subsequent discussion may be analysed in terms of a
coding scheme that allows one to categorize various aspects
of mother–child interaction. Differences between mother–
child pairs quickly become apparent. For example, one
mother simply keeps on reiterating her preference, another
goes from one rationalizaton to another. It is extremely
doubtful that we would ever have gained an insight into
these differences by simply questioning the mothers.

In other instances the child is given tasks to perform in
the presence of the mother and we observe the way in
which the mother helps (or refrains from helping) the child.

A third aspect of the laboratory method involves the use
of systematic experimental manipulations. For instance, we

may vary the sex and age of the child, the social class of the mother, the nature of the task, and so on. Most variations in the nature of the task involve varying degrees of restriction on the behaviour of parent and child (Bell, 1964). For instance, we may give the parent strict instructions about what to do, let us say in administering a task or in leaving the child alone, and then we may observe the effect of this manipulation on the behaviour of the child which is allowed to proceed without restriction. In the case where the child is given a task by the experimenter in the presence of the parent, it is the child whose behaviour is relatively restricted, while the parent is left free to intervene or not to intervene in any way he considers appropriate. It is clear, that these methods provide considerable scope for experimental manipulation.

Needless to say, the application of experimental or quasi-experimental methods in this area raises a number of problems. The most serious of these is probably posed by the dilemma of artificiality. Behaviour in the laboratory is not the same as behaviour at home and behaviour in the presence of an observer is likely to differ considerably from behaviour in private. The mother (and often the child) is likely to be on her best behaviour in front of the experimenter. As in the case of the interview, she may be much more concerned with presenting a favourable image than with presenting a normal sample of her treatment of the child. Who has not observed the stilted ritual of playing 'good mother' and 'good child' in front of strangers?

Nevertheless, there are several factors in the experimental situation which give it a clear advantage over the interview. In the first place, it is much more difficult for the mother to 'fake' effectively. To do this in the interview, she has merely to say the right things, to do it in the laboratory she has to control her behaviour from moment to moment, perhaps for an hour or longer, and that is a far more difficult thing to do. In fact, for ordinary persons it is well-nigh impossible and within a very short time the mask is apt to slip. It is one thing to claim to be a good mother, it is quite another to behave like one, especially when the child itself is provocatively present. While nearly everyone knows the socially acceptable verbal formulae, no one has learned to observe and monitor their own behaviour so minutely as to be able to guarantee a socially desirable response most of the time. The average person simply cannot translate the usual global moral injunctions into the highly specific and apparently trivial actions that go to make up the fabric of ordinary social interaction. In an interview the mother may, for instance, claim to be warm and affectionate towards her child, but in direct interaction she may order the child about without being aware of what she is doing or of her inconsistency.

If parent and child find it more difficult to 'fake' in an experiment than in an interview, the psychologist finds it much easier. Where verbal formulation of questions is necessary, it is difficult to hide one's intent. In an interview, it is hardly possible to find out whether a woman is a warm and affectionate mother without asking her in some way and thus putting her on her guard. But in this context an experiment is essentially a way of asking questions in a disguised and indirect manner. Not knowing the exact nature of the question it becomes almost impossible for the mother to prepare an answer that is effectively slanted in the socially desirable direction. For example, the psychologist may want to know how the mother typically reacts to her child's questions, whether she gives uncertain or inconsistent replies, whether she often deals with a question by a counter-question, whether she is evasive, ignores questions, and so on. If he asks her directly, he is unlikely to get the truth. But if he asks in the context of an experiment, he simply manipulates the task situation so that the child is bound to be puzzled and to ask questions; then he records what the mother does. The mother reacts in terms of the apparent requirements of the task and remains in the dark as to the real content of the inquiry. It then becomes almost impossible for her to anticipate the socially desirable response.

While the advantages of controlled observation and manipulation are clear enough, they are purchased at the price of deception. Research of this kind does involve a degree of manipulation that becomes morally dubious. Moreover, the more successful the manipulation, the more successfully the experimental subject's privacy has been invaded. This invasion is far more real than the relatively trivial instances that occur in many social psychological experiments carried out on university students. However, in both instances the experimenter feels that the search for the truth entitles him to take certain liberties he will not take when he steps out of the research role. The core of the social psychologist's dilemma lies precisely in this – that he must either allow himself to be fooled by people's natural tendency to hide the truth or he must fool his subjects into giving themselves away. Putting the problem in less blunt language will only add self-deception to the deception practised on his experimental subjects.

What then are the alternatives? One could return to interview methods and give the subject a fair chance to defend himself and hide the truth. But that would clearly be folly. Or one could renounce research in this area. But if there is a chance of improving the quality of human relationships by prying into them to learn the truth, are we not obliged to pry? Perhaps the propriety of the means should be judged also in terms of the ends they serve. But this is a dangerous equation and the individual investigator may easily be led astray by his own scientific commitments. It would be as well to submit such judgements to special tribunals set up for the purpose, a development that has in fact occurred in a number of research centres. To pursue these problems further would take us far beyond the context of this volume for which it is in fact more appropriate to ask whether the moral dilemma cannot be avoided by the use of alternative techniques.

Method and theory

In the clinical setting it is supposedly the interests of the patient and not those of the psychologist which determine what happens. Any general insights which the psychologist gains in the course of clinical observation and practice are simply by-products of his primary concern with the welfare of the patient. It is the latter which sets severe limits for any attempts at control and manipulation of conditions that might be suggested by scientific curiosity. Morever, the possible therapeutic benefit represents a kind of repayment for the more serious invasion of privacy that the patient suffers.

The scientific disadvantges of clinical case study require no elaboration. It is obviously not a technique that can be used to test the validity of generalizations about human behaviour, because of the unknown and largely uncontrolled effects of intervention by the clinician. Moreover, Freud's view that the therapeutic effectiveness of a therapist has nothing to do with the validity of his theoretical generalizations is by now a commonplace. Nevertheless, the clinical method remains a valuable *source* of general hypotheses about socialization, hypotheses which then require to be tested in other contexts. It is sometimes forgotten that the development of a sound theory requires the *generation* of good hypotheses as well as their testing. As the number of possible hypotheses for the explanation of human behaviour is probably infinite, their rigorous testing can become an extremely wasteful process, unless they reach some level of initial plausibility. It does seem reasonable to suppose that generalizations which have already proved their worth in understanding individual cases are better candidates for experimental testing than generalizations that have been sucked out of someone's theoretical thumb. The literature on socialization is full of rather fruitless attempts to test hypotheses that had little claim to initial plausibility.

In one sense, of course, clinical generalizations are *never* tested experimentally. What the clinician often does is to provide a historical narrative (Sherwood, 1969) of an individual case, a particular family, for example. This narrative, which may or may not be couched in psychoanalytic language, provides an understanding of a peculiar union of circumstances. The determination of the precise *conditions* under which any particular set of clinical concepts is applicable becomes a matter for quasi-experimental investigation and leaves untouched the question of the pragmatic usefulness of these concepts in any particular instance. In the extreme case, it is possible to imagine an explanation that is uniquely applicable to only a single parent–child dyad. Phenomenologists, in fact, show a preference for this type of explanation. So far, however, their incursions into the field of socialization have mainly been based on reconstructions of the past by adult patients and while the retrospective creation of a personal history is of great intrinsic interest it has very little to do with what actually happened and is at best of marginal interest to the student of socialization.

At the other extreme, there are studies of 'social reinforcement' whose relevance to the study of socialization remains equally questionable (Baldwin, 1967, ch. 16). In this case, the problem is not one of narrow particularity but of a generality that is so extreme as to let almost the entire subject matter of socialization drop through the wide meshes of its net. Significance and triviality should not be thought of as the opposite ends of a line but as the opposite poles of a sphere, so that if we start at one pole we can reach the other pole equally well by facing in opposite directions. We can reach the ultimate point of triviality either by becoming more and more particular or by becoming more and more general. In the one case, we end up by saying nothing of general significance; in the other case, we end up with statements that are so general as to apply to almost anything and hence lose their original significance.

This problem becomes particularly acute when attempts are made to use terms like 'social reinforcement' for the explanation of behaviour changes in natural settings. For example, in one fairly well-known study the behaviour of a four-year-old boy in nursery school was changed by a psychologist who stayed close to him for long periods and attended solely to him (Scott, Burton and Yarrow, 1967). Every time the boy did something that was judged worthy of approval, there would be exclamations of 'That's fine', smiling, nodding, moving closer, etc. Of course, the approved behaviour became more frequent in the presence of the psychologist and notably less frequent within a few days of the latter's departure.

One may choose to ascribe the outcome of such an intervention to the operation of something called 'social reinforcement'. The scientistic sound of this term may lead one to believe that a discovery has been made, an explanation found, a theory validated, when in fact all the questions raised by everyday observation of human interaction remain unanswered. We do not know what exactly has changed the boy's behaviour, nor do we know anything about the nature of the change. Probably, he was delighted by the special attention he received in relation to the other children and tried to perpetuate this pleasant state of affairs. By behaving appropriately, he was hoping to manipulate the situation so as to achieve this aim. When it did not work he lost interest. The so-called social reinforcement paradigm adds nothing to our information about what situations children like – for that we still have to rely on naïve experience. Furthermore, the 'surplus meaning' it carries over from laboratory studies may actually blind us to the really important human factors in the situation and tempt us to think of reinforcement in terms of isolated bits of behaviour like offering food pellets, sweets or head nods. Outside the laboratory, reinforcing properties are, of course, much more likely to inhere in social constellations than in separate acts of approval or attention. Such acts merely express a social situation; they are meaningless in isolation.

Such considerations lead to general questions about the

role of the experimental method in socialization research. An experiment in social psychology involves the artificial creation of a human situation. As such, it has more in common with the theatre than is generally realized. The investigator carefully chooses his stage props, prepares a script and chooses his actors. The script may or may not leave more room for individual variation than the average theatre script. Questions are asked about the effect of known variations in script and props on the presentation made by one or more of the actors. It is hoped that the production will simulate some real-life problem or situation, but there, is of course, no guarantee that it will do so.

Like the theatre, experiments are constantly pulled in two directions. On the one hand, there are the demands of relevance to the human situation outside the playhouse or the laboratory; on the other hand, there are the demands of the medium and its tradition. The canons of the rigorous experiment are in some ways reminiscent of the canons of classical drama – they demand a purity of form which is more likely to be aesthetically than humanly satisfying. Each of the requirements of rigorous experimentation sets limits to the validity of its findings in non-experimental settings.

For socialization research, the major problem that arises in connection with the demand for experimental control is the problem of the anonymity of the socialization agent. In real life, the agents of socialization are persons with a specific social identity; they are mother, father, teacher, and so on. That is to say, they have a definite place in the world and in relation to the child. In an experiment, the source of the social influence to which the child is exposed is more or less anonymous, or at best sketchily identified by sex and age. The reason for this lies in the greater possibility for manipulating the behaviour of experimenter's stooges, used as stimulus persons. Using strangers as social stimuli also allows one to control the history of their relationship with the child. Undoubtedly, there are some general principles in all learning from human models. But we should be prepared for the possibility that in real-life relationships with parents and teachers these general principles account for only a small part of the variance. In any case, there is no way to find out, except by empirical studies, using socialization agents that have a genuine identity, like the child's own parents. It is unfortunate that such studies are rare.

It is instructive to note a crucial difference between the goal of experiments involving parents and children, and conventional social psychological experiments on individual behaviour in small groups (Haley, 1967). In the latter case, the choice of experimental subjects is generally limited to those who have no pre-experimental history of association with one another; this enables the experimenter to ascribe changes in behaviour to the influence of the manipulated experimental setting. In experiments on parents and children, on the contrary, the problem is to eliminate the special effect of the experimental situation as much as possible, so that their historically determined, typical pattern of interaction may emerge.

Another example of the way in which extraneous traditions of experimental design have limited the use of certain theoretical models is to be found in the distinction between independent and dependent variables. The former are the factors that the experimenter manipulates, the latter are the observed consequences of this manipulation. Psychological experiments are almost invariably governed by a strict distinction between these two sets of variables, and experiments in the field of social learning are no exception. Underlying this distinction we will find an implicit simplistic belief in the separability of causes and effects. In the psychological experiment, causes are usually identified with antecedents and effects with consequents, causation being seen only in terms of temporal succession. Quite often, the words stimulus and response are substituted for the terms antecedent and consequent, a usage which represents a far cry from the original, more precise, meaning of these terms. In the typical social learning experiment the child's behaviour will be seen as a consequence of the prior manipulations performed by the experimenter.

But outside the laboratory the distinction between independent and dependent variables does not exist and the distinction between antecedents and consequents breaks down. In a sequence of social interaction it is hardly possible and certainly not helpful to differentiate clearly between events called antecedents and events called consequents. What we have is a succession of events which mutually influence each other in the course of time. Parent and child interact and the direction of causal effects goes both ways. Approaching this situation with the paradigm of the psychological experiment in mind, we are likely to see the parent as the incarnation of the stimulus element and the child as the incarnation of the response element. This does not advance our correct understanding of the situation.

In order to study such an interaction it is necessary to drop the distinction between independent and dependent variables and to treat each as dependent on the other. In the usual laboratory situation this would be inappropriate, as the possible effect of the child on the experimenter is excluded by definition. However, in observations of parents and children, the behaviour of both needs to be recorded to get a picture of what is going on. It may also be necessary to introduce much longer time periods than are usual in laboratory experiments. It would still be possible to introduce artificial variations in the conditions of interaction, but the greatest need at present is for careful observation of the interaction of parents and children. Parents and children form a system with inputs in the form of external constraints and outputs in the form of more or less stable psychological effects. This system is not a 'black box' – we need but look and listen closely to find out how it works.

References

AINSWORTH, M. (1969), 'Object relations, dependency and attachment: a theoretical review of the infant–mother relationship', *Child Devel.*, vol. 40, pp. 969–1025.

AINSWORTH, M., and SALTER, D. (1963), 'The development of infant–mother interaction among the Ganda', in B. M. Foss (ed.), *Determinants of Infant Behaviour*, vol. 2, Methuen.

AINSWORTH, M., SALTER, D., and WITTIG, B. A. (1967), 'Attachment and exploratory behaviour of one year olds in a strange situation', in B. M. Foss (ed.), *Determinants of Infant Behaviour*, vol. 4, Methuen.

ALLINSMITH, W. (1960), 'The learning of moral standards', in D. R. Miller and G. E. Swanson (eds.), *Inner Conflict and Defense*, Holt, Rinehart & Winston.

ARIES, P. (1962), *Centuries of Childhood*, Cape.

ARONFREED, J. (1961), 'The nature, variety and social patterning of moral responses to transgression', *J. abnorm. soc. Psychol.*, vol. 63, pp. 223–40.

ARONFREED, J. (1969), 'The concept of internalization', in D. A. Goslin (ed.), *Handbook of Socialization Theory and Research*, Rand McNally.

BAILYN, L. (1959), 'Mass media and children: a study of exposure habits and cognitive effects', *Psychol. Monogr.*, vol. 73, no. 471.

BALDWIN, A. L. (1967), *Theories of Child Development*, Wiley.

BANDURA, A. (1965a), 'Vicarious processes: a case of no-trial learning', in L. Berkowitz (ed.), *Advances in Experimental Social Psychology*, vol. 2, Academic Press.

BANDURA, A. (1965b), 'Influence of models' reinforcement contingencies on the acquisition of imitative responses', *J. Person. soc. Psychol.*, vol. 1, pp. 589–95.

BANDURA, A. (1969), *Principles of Behavioral Modification*, Holt, Rinehart & Winston.

BANDURA, A., and WALTERS, R. H. (1960), *Adolescent Aggression*, Ronald Press.

BANDURA, A., GRUSEC, J. E., and MENLOVE, J. L. (1967), 'Some social determinants of self-monitoring reinforcement systems', *J. Person. soc. Psychol.*, vol. 5, pp. 449–55.

BANDURA, A., ROSS, D., and ROSS, S. A. (1963a), 'Imitation of film mediated aggressive models', *J. abnorm. soc. Psychol.*, vol. 66, pp. 3–11.

BANDURA, A., ROSS, D., and ROSS, S. A. (1963b), 'A comparative test of the status envy, social power and secondary reinforcement theories of identificatory learning', *J. abnorm. soc. Psychol.*, vol. 67, pp. 527–34.

BARRY, H., CHILD, I. L., and BACON, M. K. (1959), 'Relations of child training to subsistence economy', *Amer. Anthrop.*, vol. 61, pp. 51–63.

BATESON, G., JACKSON, D., HALEY, J., and WEAKLAND, J. (1956), 'Toward a theory of schizophrenia', *Behav. Sci.*, vol. 1, pp. 251–64.

BAUMRIND, D. (1966), 'Effects of authoritative parental controls on child behavior', *Child Devel.*, vol. 37, pp. 887–907.

BECKER, W. C. (1964), 'Consequences of different kinds of parental discipline', in M. L. Hoffman and L. W. Hoffman (eds.), *Review of Child Development Research*, vol. 1, Russell Sage Foundation, New York.

BELL, R. Q. (1964), 'Structuring parent–child interaction situations for direct observation', *Child Devel.*, vol. 35, pp. 1009–20.

BELL, R. Q. (1968), 'A reinterpretation of the direction of effects in studies of socialization', *Psychol. Rev.*, vol. 75, pp. 81–95.

BELOFF, H. (1957), 'The structure and origin of the anal character', *Genet. psychol. Monogr.*, vol. 55, pp. 141–72.

BERNSTEIN, B. (1964), 'Elaborated and restricted codes: their social origins and some consequences', *Amer. Anthrop.*, vol. 66, no. 6, part 2, pp. 55–69.

BERRIEN, F. K. (1967), 'Methodological and related problems in cross-cultural research', *Int. J. Psychol.*, vol. 2, pp. 33–43.

BIEBER, I., *et al.* (1962), *Homosexuality*, Basic Books.

BIJOU, S. W. (1970), 'Reinforcement history and socialization', in R. A. Hoppe, G. A. Milton and E. C. Simmel (eds.), *Early Experiences and the Processes of Socialization*, Academic Press.

BING, E. (1963), 'Effects of childrearing practices on development of differential cognitive abilities', *Child Devel.*, vol. 34, pp. 631–48; Penguin, 1971.

BOWLBY, J. (1969), *Attachment and Loss*, vol. 1, Hogarth Press; Penguin, 1971.

BRIM, O. G. (1958), 'Family structure and sex role learning by children', *Sociometry*, vol. 21, pp. 1–16.

BRONFENBRENNER, U. (1958a), 'The study of identification through interpersonal perception', in R. Tagiuri and L. Petrullo (eds.), *Person Perception and Interpersonal Behavior*, Stanford University Press.

BRONFENBRENNER, U. (1958b), 'Socialization and social class through time and space', in E. Maccoby, T. M. Newcomb and E. L. Hartley (eds.), *Readings in Social Psychology*, Holt, Rinehart & Winston.

BRONFENBRENNER, U. (1961a), 'The changing American child', *J. soc. Issues*, vol. 17, pp. 6–18.

BRONFENBRENNER, U. (1961b), 'Some familial antecedents of responsibility and leadership in adolescents', in L. Petrullo and B. M. Bass (eds.), *Leadership and Interpersonal Behavior*, Holt, Rinehart & Winston.

BROOKS, R., BRANDT, L., and WIENER, M. (1969), 'Differential response to two communication channels: socio-economic class differences in response to verbal reinforcers communicated with and without tonal inflection', *Child Devel.*, vol. 40, pp. 453–70.

BURTON, R. V. (1963), 'The generality of honesty reconsidered', *Psychol. Rev.*, vol. 70, pp. 481–500.

CAMPBELL, J. D. (1964), 'Peer relations in early childhood', in M. L. Hoffman and L. W. Hoffman (eds.), *Review of Child Development Research*, vol. 1, Russell Sage Foundation, New York.

CHOMBART DE LAUWE, M. J. (1970), 'Child representation in contemporary French urban society', in K. Danziger (ed.), *Readings in Child Socialization*, Pergamon.

CLAUSEN, J. A. (1966), 'Family structure, socialization and personality', in M. L. Hoffman and L. W. Hoffman (eds.), *Review of Child Development Research*, vol. 2, Russell Sage Foundation, New York.

CLAUSEN, J. A. (1968), *Socialization and Society*, Little, Brown.

CLAUSEN, J. A., and WILLIAMS, J. R. (1963), 'Sociological correlates of child behavior', in H. Stevenson (ed.), *Child Psychology. 62nd Yearbook of the National Society for the Study of Education*, University of Chicago Press.

COLEMAN, J. S. (1961), *The Adolescent Society*, Free Press.

COOPERSMITH, S. (1967), *The Antecedents of Self-Esteem*, W. H. Freeman.

COX, F. N., and CAMPBELL, D. (1968), 'Young children in a new situation with and without their mothers', *Child Devel.*, vol. 39, pp. 123–31.

DEUTSCH, C. P., and DEUTSCH, M. (1968), 'Brief reflections on the theory of early childhood enrichment programs', in R. D. Hess and R. M. Bear (eds.), *Early Education*, Aldine.

EISENSTADT, S. N. (1956), *From Generation to Generation*, Free Press.

ELDER, G. H., and BOWERMAN, C. E. (1963), 'Family structure and child-rearing patterns: the effect of family size and sex composition', *Amer. soc. Rev.*, vol. 28, pp. 891–905.

ELKIN, F., and WESTLEY, W. A. (1955), 'The myth of adolescent culture', *Amer. soc. Rev.*, vol. 20, p. 580.

EMMERICH, W. (1964), 'Continuity and stability in early social development', *Child Develop.*, vol. 35, pp. 311–32.

ERIKSON, E. H. (1950), *Childhood and Society*, Norton.

ERON, L. D., WALDER, L. O., TOIGO, R., and LEFKOWITZ, M. M. (1963), 'Social class, parental punishment for aggression, and child aggression', *Child Devel.*, vol. 34, pp. 849–67.

ESCALONA, S., and HEIDER, G. M. (1959), *Prediction and Outcome: A Study in Child Development*, Basic Books.

FARBER, B. (1962), 'Marital integration as a factor in parent–child relations', *Child Devel.*, vol. 33, pp. 1–14.

FESHBACH, S. (1970), 'Aggression', in P. H. Mussen (ed.), *Carmichael's Manual of Child Psychology*, vol. 2, Wiley, 3rd edn.

FLECK, S., LIDZ, T., and CORNELISON, A. (1963), 'Comparison of parent–child relationships of male and female schizophrenic patients', *Arch. gen. Psychiat.*, vol 8, pp. 1–7.

FREEBERG, N., and PAYNE, D. T. (1967), 'Parental influence on cognitive development in early childhood: a review', *Child Devel.*, vol. 38, pp. 65–88.

FREUD, A. (1937), *The Ego and the Mechanisms of Defence*, Hogarth Press.

FREUD, S. (1933), *New Introductory Lectures on Psychoanalysis*, Hogarth Press, 1949.

FRIJDA, N., and JAHODA, G. (1966), 'On the scope and methods of cross-cultural research', *Int. J. Psychol.*, vol. 1, pp. 109–27.

GEWIRTZ, J. L. (1969), 'Mechanisms of social learning: some roles of stimulation and behavior in early human development', in D. A. Goslin (ed.), *Handbook of Socialization Theory and Research*, Rand McNally.

GORANSON, R. E. (1969), 'A review of recent literature on psychological effects of media portrayals of violence', in D. L. Lange, R. K. Baker and S. J. Ball (eds.), *Mass Media and Violence*, vol. 11. Report to the National Commission on the Causes and Prevention of Violence, US Government, Washington.

GREENGLASS, E. R. (1971), 'A cross-cultural study of the relationship between resistance to temptation and maternal communication', *Genet. psychol. Monogr.*, in press.

HAGGARD, E. A., BREKSTAD, A., and SKARD, A. G. (1960), 'On the reliability of the anamnestic interview', *J. abnorm. soc. Psychol.*, vol. 61, pp. 311–18.

HALEY, J. (1959), 'The family of the schizophrenic: a model system', *J. nerv. ment. Dis.*, vol. 129, pp. 357–74.

HALEY, J. (1967), 'Family experiments: a new type of experimentation', in G. Handel (ed.), *The Psychosocial Interior of the Family*, Aldine.

HAMPSON, J. L. (1965), 'Determinants of psychosexual orientation', in F. A. Beach (ed.), *Sex and Behavior*, Wiley.

HARLOW, H. F., and HARLOW, M. K. (1965), 'The affectional systems', in A. M. Schrier, H. F. Harlow and F. Stollnitz (eds.), *Behavior of Non-Human Primates*, Academic Press.

HARTSHORNE, H., and MAY, M. A. (1928–30), *Studies in the Nature of Character*, Macmillan Co.

HARVEY, O. J., *et al.* (1966), 'Teachers' belief systems and preschool atmospheres', *J. educ. Psychol.*, vol. 57, pp. 373–81.

HEIDER, F. (1958), *The Psychology of Interpersonal Relations*, Wiley.

HELLMAN, I. (1962), 'Sudden separation and its effect followed over twenty years: Hampstead Nursery follow-up studies', *Psychoanal. Stud. Child*, vol. 17, pp. 159–74.

HENRY, J. (1963), *Culture against Man*, Random House.

HESS, R. D. (1970), 'Social class and ethnic influences on socialization', in P. H. Mussen (ed.), *Carmichael's Manual of Child Psychology*, vol. 2, Wiley, 3rd edn.

HESS, R. D., and SHIPMAN, V. C. (1965), 'Early experience and the socialization of cognitive modes in children', *Child Devel.*, vol. 36, pp. 869–86.

HESS, R. D., and SHIPMAN, V. C. (1967), 'Cognitive elements in maternal behavior', in J. P. Hill (ed.), *Minnesota Symposia on Child Psychology*, vol. 1, University of Minnesota Press.

HETHERINGTON, E. M. (1965), 'A developmental study of the effects of sex of the dominant parent on sex-role preference, identification and imitation in children', *J. Person. soc. Psychol.*, vol. 2, pp. 188–94.

HIMMELWEIT, H. T., OPPENHEIM, A. N., and VINCE, P. (1958), *Television and the Child*, Oxford University Press.

HOFFMAN, M. (1969), 'Moral development', in P. H. Mussen (ed.), *Manual of Child Psychology*, Wiley.

HOFFMAN, M., and SALTZSTEIN, H. (1967), 'Parent discipline and the child's moral development', *J. Person. soc. Psychol.*, vol. 5, pp. 45–57.

HONZIK, M. P. (1967), 'Environmental correlates of mental growth: prediction from the family setting at twenty-one months', *Child Devel.*, vol. 38, pp. 337–64.

HSU, F. L. K., WATROUS, B. G., and LORD, E. M. (1960–61), 'Culture pattern and adolescent behavior', *Int. J. soc. Psychiat.*, vol. 7, pp. 33–5.

KAGAN, J. (1967), 'On the need for relativism', *Amer. Psychol.*, vol. 22, pp. 131–42.

KAGAN, J. (1969), 'The three faces of continuity in human development', in D. A. Goslin (ed.), *Handbook of Socialization Theory and Research*, Rand McNally.

KAGAN, J., and MOSS, H. A. (1962), *Birth to Maturity*, Wiley.

KAMII, C. K., and RADIN, N. L. (1967), 'Class differences in the socialization practices of Negro mothers', *J. Marr. Fam.*, vol. 29, pp. 302–10.

KARDINER, A., (1945), *The Psychological Frontiers of Society*, Columbia University Press.

KARR, C., and WESLEY, F. (1966), 'Comparison of German and US child-rearing practices', *Child Devel.*, vol. 37, pp. 715–23.

KATCHER, A. (1965), 'The discrimination of sex differences by young children', *J. genet. Psychol.*, vol. 87, pp. 131–43.

KENISTON, K. (1960), *The Uncommitted: Alienated Youth in American Society*, Harcourt, Brace & World.

KENISTON, K. (1968), *Young Radicals: Notes on Committed Youth*, Harcourt, Brace & World.

KOGAN, N., and WALLACH, M. A. (1964), *Risk Taking: A Study in Cognition and Personality*, Holt, Rinehart & Winston.

KOHLBERG, L. (1963a), 'The development of children's orientations toward a moral order: I. Sequence in the development of moral thought', *Vita Humana*, vol. 6, pp. 11–33.

KOHLBERG, L. (1963b), 'Moral development and identification', in H. W. Stevenson (ed.), *Child Psychology. 62nd Yearbook of the National Society for the Study of Education*, University of Chicago Press.

KOHLBERG, L. (1964), 'Development of moral character and moral ideology', in M. L. Hoffman and L. W. Hoffman (eds.), *Review of Child Development Research*, vol. 1, Russell Sage Foundation, New York.

KOHLBERG, L. (1966), 'A cognitive-developmental analysis of children's sex-role concepts and attitudes', in E. E. Maccoby (ed.), *The Development of Sex Differences*, Stanford University Press.

KOHLBERG, L. (1969), 'Stage and sequence: the cognitive-developmental approach to socialization', in D. A. Goslin (ed.), *Handbook of Socialization Theory and Research*, Rand McNally.

KOHLBERG, L., and ZIGLER, E. (1967), 'The impact of cognitive maturity on sex-role attitudes in the years four to eight', *Genet. psychol. Monogr.*, vol. 75, pp. 89–165.

KOHN, M. L. (1959), 'Social class and parental values', *Amer. J. Sociol.*, vol. 64, pp. 337–51.

KOHN, M. L. (1963), 'Social class and parent–child relationships: an interpretation', *Amer. J. Sociol.*, vol. 68, pp. 471–80.

KOHN, M. L. (1969), *Class and Conformity: A Study in Values*, Dorsey Press.

KURTH, E. (1964), 'Fernsehen und Verhaltensstorungen', *Z. Psychol.*, vol. 170, pp. 261–9.

LAING, R. D. (1961), *The Self and Others*, Tavistock.

LARSEN, O., GRAY, L., and FORTAS, J. (1968), 'Achieving goals through violence on television', in O. Larsen (ed.), *Violence in the Mass Media*, Harper & Row.

LASKO, J. K. (1954), 'Parent behavior toward first and second children', *Genet. psychol. Monogr.*, vol. 49, pp. 97–137.

LAZARUS, R. S. (1966), *Psychological Stress and the Coping Process*. McGraw-Hill.

LENNARD, H., BEAULIEU, M. R., and EMBREY, N. G. (1965), 'Interaction in families with a schizophrenic child', *Arch. gen. Psychiat.*, vol. 12, pp. 166–83.

LEVY, D. M. (1958), *Behavioral Analysis: Analysis of Clinical Observations of Behavior as Applied to Mother–Newborn Relationships*, C. C. Thomas.

LEWIN, K. (1935), *A Dynamic Theory of Personality*, McGraw-Hill.

MACCOBY, E. E. (1964), 'Effects of the mass media', in M. L. Hoffman and L. W. Hoffman (eds.), *Review of Child Development Research*, vol. 1, Russell Sage Foundation, New York.

MCCORD, J., and MCCORD, W. (1961), 'Cultural stereotypes and the validity of interviews for research in child development', *Child Devel.*, vol. 32, pp. 171–85.

MCCORD, W., MCCORD, J., and HOWARD, A. (1961), 'Familial correlates of aggression in nondelinquent male children', *J. abnorm. soc. Psychol.*, vol. 62, pp. 79–93.

MASLOW, A. H., and DIAZ-GUERRERO, R. (1960), 'Delinquency as a value disturbance', in J. G. Peatman and E. L. Hartley (eds.), *Festschrift for Gardner Murphy*, Harper & Row.

MEAD, M. (1956), *New Lives for Old*, Morrow.

MILNER, E. (1951), 'A study of the relationship between reading readiness in grade one school children and patterns of parent–child interaction', *Child Devel.*, vol. 22, pp. 95–112.

MINTURN, L., and LAMBERT, W. W. (1964), *Mothers of Six Cultures*, Wiley.

MISCHEL, W. (1970), 'Sex-typing and socialization', in P. H. Mussen (ed.), *Carmichael's Manual of Child Psychology*, vol. 2, Wiley, 3rd edn.

MISCHEL, W., and GRUSEC, J. (1966), 'Determinants of the rehearsal and transmission of neutral and aversive behaviors', *J. Person. soc. Psychol.*, vol. 2, pp. 197–205.

MISHLER, E. G., and WAXLER, N. E. (1968), *Interaction in Families*, Wiley.

MOSS, H. A. (1967), 'Sex, age and state as determinants of mother–infant interaction', *Merrill-Palmer Q.*, vol. 13, pp. 19–36.

MUSSEN, P., and RUTHERFORD, E. (1963), 'Parent–child relations and parental personality in relation to young children's sex-role preferences', *Child Devel.*, vol. 34, pp. 581–607.

PECK, R. F., and HAVIGHURST, R. J. (1960), *The Psychology of Character Development*, Wiley.

PETERSON, D. R., and MIGLIORINO, G. (1967), 'The uses and limitations of factor analysis in cross-cultural research on socialization', *Int. J. Psychol.*, vol. 2, pp. 215–20.

PIAGET, J. (1932), *The Moral Judgement of the Child*, Routledge & Kegan Paul.

PIAGET, J. (1951), *Play, Dreams and Imitation in Childhood*, Heinemann.

REED, M. R., and ASBJORNSEN, W. (1968), 'Experimental alteration of the It Scale in the study of sex-role preference', *Percept. mot. Skills*, vol. 26, pp. 15–24.

RHEINGOLD, H. L. (1968), 'Infancy', *International Encyclopaedia of the Social Sciences*, Macmillan Co.

ROBBINS, L. C. (1963), 'The accuracy of parental recall of aspects of child development and of child rearing practices', *J. abnorm. soc. Psychol.*, vol. 66, pp. 261–70.

ROBINSON, W. P., and RACKSTRAW, S. J. (1967), 'Variations in mothers' answers to children's questions, as a function of social class, verbal intelligence test scores and sex', *Sociology*, vol. 1, pp. 259–76.

ROSENBERG, M. (1965), *Society and the Adolescent Self-Image*, Princeton University Press.

ROSENBLATT, J. S. (1965), 'The basis of synchrony in the behavioural interaction between the mother and her offspring in the laboratory rat', in B. M. Foss (ed.), *Determinants of Infant Behaviour*, vol. 3, Methuen.

ROSENHAN, D. L. (1966), 'Effects of social class and race on responsiveness to approval and disapproval', *J. Person. soc. Psychol.*, vol. 4, pp. 253–9.

ROSENHAN, D. L., and GREENWALD, J. (1965), 'The effects of age, sex and socioeconomic class on responsiveness to two classes of verbal reinforcement', *J. Person.* vol. 33, pp. 108–21.

RUBIN, K. H., HULTSCH, D. F., and PETERS, D. L. (1971), 'Non-social speech in four-year-old children as a function of birth order and inter-personal situation', *Merrill-Palmer Q.*, vol. 17, pp. 41–50.

RYERSON, A. J. (1961), 'Medical advice on child-rearing, 1550–1900', *Harv. educ. Rev.*, vol. 31, pp. 302–33.

SAMPSON, E. E. (1965), 'The study of ordinal position: antecedents and outcomes', in B. A. Maher (ed.), *Progress in Experimental Personality Research*, vol. 2, Academic Press.

SCHAEFER, E. S. (1959), 'A circumplex model for maternal behavior', *J. abnorm. soc. Psychol.*, vol. 59, pp. 226–35.

SCHAEFER, E. S., and BAYLEY, N. (1963), 'Maternal behaviour, child behaviour and their interaction from infancy through adolescence', *Monogr. Soc. Res. Child Devel.*, vol. 28, no. 87.

SCHAFFER, H. R., and EMERSON, P. E. (1964), 'The development of social attachments in infancy', *Monogr. Soc. Res. Child Devel.*, vol. 29, no. 30.

SCOTT, J. P. (1968), *Early Experience and the Organization of Behavior*, Wadsworth.

SCOTT, P., BURTON, R. V., and YARROW, M. R. (1967), 'Social reinforcement under natural conditions', *Child Devel.*, vol. 38, pp. 53–63.

SEARS, R. R., MACCOBY, E. E., and LEVIN, H. (1957), *Patterns of Child Rearing*, Row, Peterson.

SEARS, R. R., RAU, L., and ALPERT, R. (1965), *Identification and Child Rearing*, Stanford University Press.

SHERWOOD, M. (1969), *The Logic of Explanation in Psycho-Analysis*, Academic Press.

SIEGEL, A. E., and HAAS, M. B. (1963), 'The working mother: a review of research', *Child Devel.*, vol. 34, pp. 513–42.

SOLOMON, R. L. (1964), 'Punishment', *Amer. Psychol.*, vol. 19, pp. 239–53.

SPENCE, J. T., and SEGNER, L. L. (1967), 'Verbal versus nonverbal reinforcement combinations in the discrimination learning of middle- and lower-class children', *Child Devel.*, vol. 38, pp. 29–38.

STEVENSON, H. W. (1965), 'Social reinforcement of children's behavior', in L. P. Lipsitt and C. C. Spiker (eds.), *Advances in Child Development and Behavior*, vol. 2, Academic Press.

THOMAS, A. (1963), *Behavioral Individuality in Early Childhood*, New York University Press.

VERNON, P. E. (1964), *Personality Assessment*, Methuen.

WALTERS, E., and CRANDALL, V. J. (1964), 'Social class and observed maternal behavior from 1940 to 1960', *Child Devel.*, vol. 35, pp. 1021–32.

WALTERS, R. H., and PARKE, R. D. (1965), 'The role of the distance receptors in the development of social responsiveness', in L. P. Lipsitt and C. C. Spiker (eds.), *Advances in Child Development and Behavior*, vol. 2, Academic Press.

WALTERS, R. H., and THOMAS, E. L. (1963), 'Enhancement of punitiveness by visual and audio-visual displays', *Canad. J. Psychol.*, vol. 17, pp. 244–55.

WHITING, J. W. M. (1954), 'The cross-cultural method', in G. Lindzey (ed.), *Handbook of Social Psychology*, Addison-Wesley.

WHITING, J. W. M. (1960), 'Resource mediation and learning by identification', in I. Iscoe and H. W. Stevenson (eds.), *Personality Development in Children*, University of Texas Press.

WINCH, R. J. (1962), *Identification and its Familial Determinants*, Bobbs-Merrill.

WOLFENSTEIN, M. (1953), 'Trends in infant care', *Amer. J. Orthopsychiat.*, vol. 23, pp. 120–30.

WRIGHT, H. F. (1956), 'Psychological development in the Midwest', *Child Devel.*, vol. 27, pp. 265–86.

WRONG, D. (1961), 'The oversocialized conception of man in modern sociology', *Amer. soc. Rev.*, vol. 26, pp. 183–93.

WYNNE, L.C., RYCKOFF, I., DAY, J., and HIRSCH, S. (1958), 'Pseudo-mutuality in the family relations of schizophrenics', *Psychiatry*, vol. 21, pp. 205–20.

YARROW, L. J. (1964), 'Separation from parents during early childhood', in M. L. Hoffman and L. W. Hoffman (eds.), *Review of Child Development Research*, vol. 1, Russell Sage Foundation, New York.

YARROW, M. R., CAMPBELL, J. D., and BURTON, R. V. (1964), 'Reliability of maternal retrospection: a preliminary report', *Family Process*, vol. 3, pp. 207–18. Reprinted in K. Danziger (ed.), *Readings in Child Socialization*, Pergamon, 1970.

YARROW, M. R., CAMPBELL, J. D., and BURTON, R. V. (1968), *Child Rearing: An Inquiry into Research and Methods*, Jossey-Bass, San Francisco.

YOUNG, F. W. (1962), 'The function of male initiation ceremonies: a cross-cultural test of an alternative hypothesis', *Amer. J. Sociol.*, vol. 67, pp. 379–96.

ZIGLER, E., and CHILD, I. L. (1969), 'Socialization', in G. Lindzey and E. Aronson (eds.), *Handbook of Social Psychology*, vol. 3. Addison-Wesley, 2nd edn.

ZIGLER, E., and DELABRY, J. (1962), 'Concept-switching in middle-class, lower-class and retarded children', *J. abnorm. soc. Psychol.*, vol. 65, pp. 267–73.

ZUNICH, M. (1961), 'A study of relationships between child-rearing attitudes and maternal behavior', *J. exp. Educ.*, vol. 30, pp. 231–41.

Index